Keynotes in Criminology and Criminal Justice Series

CYBERCRIME

Peter Grabosky, Ph.D.
Australian National University, Canberra

New York   Oxford
OXFORD UNIVERSITY PRESS

Oxford University Press is a department of the University of Oxford.
It furthers the University's objective of excellence in research,
scholarship, and education by publishing worldwide.

Oxford   New York
Auckland   Cape Town   Dar es Salaam   Hong Kong   Karachi
Kuala Lumpur   Madrid   Melbourne   Mexico City   Nairobi
New Delhi   Shanghai   Taipei   Toronto

With offices in
Argentina   Austria   Brazil   Chile   Czech Republic   France   Greece
Guatemala   Hungary   Italy   Japan   Poland   Portugal   Singapore
South Korea   Switzerland   Thailand   Turkey   Ukraine   Vietnam

For titles covered by Section 112 of the US Higher Education
Opportunity Act, please visit www.oup.com/us/he for the
latest information about pricing and alternate formats.

Published by Oxford University Press
198 Madison Avenue, New York, New York 10016
http://www.oup.com

ISBN 978-0-19-021155-4

Cataloging-in-Publication Data is on file with the Library of Congress.

Printing number: 9 8 7 6 5 4 3 2 1

Printed in the United States of America
on acid-free paper

CONTENTS

Acknowledgments   iv
About the Author   vi
Preface   vii

1. Introduction   1

2. A Brief History of Cybercrime   4

3. A Typology of Computer Crime   8

4. Cybercrime Explained   55

5. Incidence, Prevalence, Distribution, and Impacts   61

6. Trends in Cybercrime   76

7. Investigation, Prosecution, and Sentencing   91

8. Conclusion: The Future of Cybercrime and Its
   Control   120

Endnotes   138
References   140
Appendix: Useful Websites Relating to Cybercrime   159
Index   161

To my teachers

———

ACKNOWLEDGMENTS

I am grateful to Taylor and Francis (www.tandfonline.com) for permission to reproduce extracts from Peter Grabosky, "The Global Dimension of Cybercrime," *Global Crime, 6* (no.1): 146–157. http://www.tandfonline.com/doi/abs/10.1080/1744057042000297034.

We would like to thank the following reviewers of this edition: Professor Stephen A. Morreale (Worcester State University) and Professor Alexander Muentz (Temple University).

Keynotes in Criminology and Criminal Justice Series

This Series is designed to provide essential knowledge on important contemporary matters of crime, law, and justice to a broad audience of readers including students, educators, researchers, and practitioners alike, and in a format that is not only authoritative, but highly engaging, and concise. Nationally and internationally respected scholars share their knowledge and unique insights in comprehensive surveys and penetrating analyses of a variety of major contemporary issues central to the study of criminology, criminal justice, and social justice more generally. Forthcoming and planned Series books cover such areas as electronic crime, race, crime and justice, white-collar and corporate crime, violence in international perspective, gender and crime, gangs, mass incarceration, police and surveillance, financial fraud, and critical criminology.

I invite you to examine the Series and see how these readable, affordable, topical, and highly informative books can be used to help educate a new generation of students in understanding the social realities surrounding crime and justice in both domestic and global perspective.

Henry N. Pontell, Editor
Keynotes in Criminology and Criminal Justice Series
Distinguished Professor, John Jay College of Criminal Justice, CUNY
Professor Emeritus, University of California, Irvine

ABOUT THE AUTHOR

Peter Grabosky is professor emeritus in the Regulatory Institutions Network, College of Asia and the Pacific, Australian National University, and a fellow of the Academy of the Social Sciences in Australia. His general interests are in harnessing nongovernmental resources in furtherance of public policy. His publications include *Cyber Criminals on Trial* (with Russell Smith and Gregor Urbas, Cambridge University Press, 2004), which won the Distinguished Book Award of the American Society of Criminology's Division of International Criminology in 2005. Other books include *Electronic Theft* (with Russell Smith and Gillian Dempsey, Cambridge University Press, 2001); and *Crime in the Digital Age* (with Russell Smith, Federation Press/Transaction Publishers, 1998). He was previously Deputy Director of the Australian Institute of Criminology. Other appointments included Russell Sage Fellow in Law and Social Science at Yale Law School (1976–1978); Visiting Expert, the United Nations Asia and Far East Institute for the Prevention of Crime and the Treatment of Offenders (1995); and Visiting Professor, Chinese People's Public Security University (1996, 2014), Chuo University (1993, 2008), University of Manchester (2011), and City University of Hong Kong (2012). He was rapporteur for the Workshop on Crimes Related to the Computer Network at the Tenth United Nations Congress on the Prevention of Crime and the Treatment of Offenders, Vienna, 2000, and leader of the Workshop on Computer Crime at the Second World Summit of Attorneys General, Prosecutors General and Chief Prosecutors, Doha, 2005. He is past president of the Australian and New Zealand Society of Criminology, and past vice-president of the Asian Criminological Society. He lives in Canberra, Australia (Peter.Grabosky@anu.edu.au).

PREFACE

Authors often incur debts in the course of writing books, and this one is no exception. I first began working in the area of computer-related crime in 1995 at the Australian Institute of Criminology. I am grateful to the then director, Adam Graycar, for encouraging me to work in the area and for supporting my work over the following six years. I was joined there at the end of 1995 by Dr. Russell Smith, and since then we have coauthored three books and a number of articles. He has been a great collaborator.

Another collaborator to whom I am indebted is Dr. Gregor Urbas of the University of Canberra, coauthor, with Russell Smith and myself, of *Cybercriminals on Trial*. Greg helped lead me into the arcane law of cybercrime jurisdiction.

I am also indebted to Professor Roderic Broadhurst, of the Australian National University, whose substantial entrepreneurial skills under the auspices of the University of Hong Kong Centre of Criminology produced two Asia Cybercrime Summits in 2001 and 2003, respectively. It was a privilege for me to have participated in both of these, which resulted in a coedited volume, *Cybercrime: The Challenge in Asia*.

I wish also to thank my former Ph.D. students and subsequent collaborators, Sascha Walkley and Lennon Chang, for their insights on theories of trust and cybercrime.

Other colleagues from whom I have learned a great deal include Yaman Akdeniz, Mamoun Alazab, Greg Austin, Susan Brenner, Steve Chon, Raymond Choo, David Décary-Hétu, Dorothy Denning, Benoît Dupont, Thomas Holt, Michael Joyce, Michael Levi, Victor Lo, Alastair MacGibbon, Mike McGuire, David Maimon, Fernando Miro, Hedi Nasheri, Nigel Phair, Donald Piragoff, Stein Schjolberg, Jackie Schneider, Bill Tafoya, David Wall, and Grant Wardlaw. Des Berwick, formerly of the Australasian Centre for Policing Research, one of the pioneers of cybercrime control, both in policy and in practice, also helped show me the way. Michael Stohl first taught me about terrorism longer ago than either of us cares to remember, and he taught me about cyberterrorism much more recently. Nikos Passas encouraged me to pursue additional matters prosecutorial.

The United Nations Asia and Far East Institute for the Prevention of Crime and the Treatment of Offenders (UNAFEI) hosted two workshops in preparation for the Tenth United Nations Congress on the Prevention of Crime and the Treatment of Offenders, and it produced a workshop on computer crime at the Congress. All of these were great learning experiences, and I am grateful to participants in these events and to successive Directors of UNAFEI, Fujiwara Toichi, Kitada Mikinao, and Tauchi Masahiro, for their hospitality.

Five years later, the Korean Institute of Criminology (KIC) hosted preparatory meetings for the Eleventh UN Congress and produced a workshop. Again, it was my privilege to participate in these events, and I thank KIC President Lee, Tae Hoon for involving me in the process.

Over the years, officers of the Computer Crime and Intellectual Property Section of the US Department of Justice, the Australian High Tech Crime Centre hosted by the Australian Federal Police, and the Canadian Ministry of Justice have all shared valuable insights with me. Recent conferences of the Asia Pacific Association of Technology and Society organized by Dr Laurie Lau have also been stimulating and informative.

I am indebted to the Regulatory Institutions Network of the Australian National University and to its Founding Father, John Braithwaite and his successors, for providing a splendid intellectual environment in which to write this book. Finally, I am also most grateful to the Series Editor, Professor Henry Pontell, formerly of the University of California, Irvine, and now of John Jay College, City University of New York, whose kind invitation to contribute, and friendly encouragement to finish the manuscript, made it all happen.

All of the above have been my teachers, and I gratefully dedicate this book to them.

Peter Grabosky
Canberra, Australia
July 2015

[1]

INTRODUCTION

Most people born after 1990 will not fully appreciate how profoundly the advent of digital technology and the interface of computing and communications have changed our lives. New technologies have dramatically enhanced the capacities of ordinary citizens. In years past it was often said that "Freedom of the press belongs to the man (sic) who owns one." The ability to communicate directly with the public was limited to media barons or to those influential citizens to whom media barons would give voice. Today, nearly anyone can have a website or the means to communicate through social media applications such as Twitter, YouTube, or Facebook. It is now possible for ordinary individuals to communicate instantaneously with millions of people, at negligible cost. Such mundane tasks as library research have been revolutionized by digital technology. Rather than leafing manually through one or more printed periodical indexes or library card catalogs, one can conduct electronic searches of databases and, in some cases, download entire articles in seconds.

Of course, these enhanced capacities may be used for good and bad purposes. Our growing dependence on digital technology means that many of the systems we depend on for communications, finance, health, transport, energy, and entertainment are vulnerable to disruption for fun or profit. And age is no impediment to offending. Digital technology provides young people with the facility to inflict unprecedented harm. Teenagers have succeeded in manipulating the price of shares on stock exchanges, shutting down air traffic control systems, disrupting large retail enterprises, penetrating the files of military bases, plucking pirated term papers out of cyberspace, and bullying their peers electronically. None of this would have been possible before 1980. Governments also

1

wield powers that were once the stuff of science fiction. They can spy on their own citizens, as well as on foreigners, regardless of their physical location. They can monitor the communications of foreign governments and their officials. They can disrupt almost any activity that is supported by digital technology.

This book provides an introductory overview of cybercrime and the means for its control. The term "cybercrime" is a label of convenience, and it refers to a wide range of crimes committed with the aid of digital technology. The terms "computer crime," "computer-related crime," and "cybercrime" will be used interchangeably throughout the book. Strictly speaking, cybercrime refers to criminal activities involving the networked environment based on the Internet and/or World Wide Web. But we will use it to refer to offences involving stand-alone computers as well.

One of the most striking aspects of crime in the digital age is its global reach. The phrase "cyberspace knows no boundaries" has become trite. To an unprecedented degree, offences may be committed from one side of the world against victims or targets physically located on the other side of the world. This, as we shall see, poses profound problems for law enforcement and prosecution authorities. Nevertheless, there are many aspects of cybercrime that are in principle no different from events on the ground, in terrestrial space, or, in the words of one prosecutor, "the meat world."

This book is intended to provide an introductory overview to the topic of cybercrime. The following chapters will provide a brief history of cybercrime and will describe the various offences than can involve digital technology. An understanding of cybercrime will then be developed by looking at it through the lens of routine activity theory, a simple but powerful form of analysis that can be applied to all types of crime. The following chapter will wrestle with the vexing problem of statistics of computer crime; at the risk of revealing its conclusions, the reader is hereby warned that computer crime is very difficult to measure. The wider social and economic impact of cybercrime is also noted in this chapter, and the reader will learn that digital technology enhances the capacity of both the citizen *and* the state. Next, a chapter on trends in cybercrime will review some of the most recent developments in the modus operandi of cybercriminals. The following chapter will look at issues that arise as cybercrime cases proceed through the criminal justice system, at the stages of investigation, prosecution, and sentencing. The concluding chapter will set out some basic principles and strategies for the prevention and control of cybercrime. Finally, both the References and Appendix were designed to contain a number of useful sources the reader may wish to consult in order to further his or her knowledge of cybercrime and its control.

[2]

A BRIEF HISTORY OF CYBERCRIME

Even a glancing look at historical developments in high-technology crime reveals that practically every new technology and every new application of that technology have been accompanied by criminal opportunities that are quickly exploited.

For example, the development of the telegraph in the nineteenth century invited interception of telegraphic communications or the transmission of deceptive information. The invention of the telephone was soon followed by its use in furtherance of criminal conspiracies. By the 1970s telecommunications technology enabled one to whistle into a telephone and obtain a connection for free, a practice colloquially known as "phreaking." Others relying on more traditional forms of access used the telephone to commit various forms of telemarketing fraud.

The advent of high-speed data processing technology in the late 1960s ushered in a new era in crime. Parker (1976), one of the first to write on the criminal applications of modern information technology, described how computers became the new tool of embezzlers and showed how programmers were able to falsify input and output data for personal financial advantage. Information systems lent themselves to corporate fraud as well. Parker's discussion of the 1973 Equity Funding scandal described how the assets of the company were artificially inflated by electronically creating 64,000 fictitious insurance policies. One of the pioneers of the use of data processing technology in the financial services industry, Bernard Madoff, concealed a massive Ponzi scheme for many years by using computer programs that generated false transactions (Henriques 2011). The new technologies of data processing were also ideally suited to high-volume, low-value crimes. Vaughan (1983) describes how a large pharmacy chain used a computer-generated double-billing scheme to overcharge governments for health insurance reimbursements.

The development of the Internet beginning in the 1960s, and its widespread use beginning in the early 1990s brought about a revolution in high-tech crime. The advent of the personal computer in the early 1980s significantly empowered individual users, for better and for worse. Unauthorized access to computer systems became something of a sport, and some of the more prominent hackers acquired folk-hero status within their subculture. Authorities in the United States were not amused, however, and began to respond forcefully with enforcement and prosecution. The spirit of the times is captured nicely in Bruce Sterling's (1992) book, *The Hacker Crackdown.*

The Internet lent itself to quick and efficient communications among users, but it was also vulnerable to misuse. The term "hacker" was initially coined to refer to individuals who would obtain unauthorized access to computer systems and then either harmlessly explore them or effect programming improvements. The term "cracker" was applied to individuals of a more malicious bent—those who would use their unauthorized access for destructive purposes, by altering or erasing data. In the fullness of time, the term "cracker" fell into disuse, with the term "hacker" embracing uninvited guests regardless of their motive.

A landmark date in the history of computer crime was November 2, 1988, when a graduate student in computer science at Cornell University, Robert Morris, wrote a computer program designed to reproduce itself across the Internet. What started out as an intellectual exercise, intended to estimate the size of the Internet, went terribly wrong. He was in other respects a very competent programmer, and the "worm" spread with great rapidity, overloading systems and bringing the Internet to the electronic equivalent of a grinding halt.

More recent developments in the history of computer crime include the increasing sophistication of viruses, the use of digital technology in the production and dissemination of child pornography, and the application of electronics to theft in its various forms (Grabosky, Smith, and Dempsey 2001). Since the turn of the century, the proliferation of digital devices and applications has created new opportunities for criminal exploitation. Social media have become tools for bullying and fraud. Online markets for illicit goods and services, from hacker tools, to drugs, to stolen credit card details, have become commonplace (Glenny 2011; Holt 2013; Ablon, Libicki, and Golay 2014). Governments have used digital technology to spy on their own citizens and those of other countries; to steal political and commercial secrets; and to damage, degrade, or destroy systems belonging to their adversaries (Greenwald 2014; Zetter 2014).

A BRIEF HISTORY OF CYBERCRIME LEGISLATION

Technology tends to develop faster than the law, and the growth of digital technology has inspired legislative efforts to catch up. Although nations differ in terms of technological development and legislative agility, it is possible to identify six historical waves of computer crime legislation (Sieber 1998).

The first, which related to issues of privacy, began in the 1970s. Recognizing that developments in information storage and retrieval were beginning to provide governments with unprecedented capacity to collect, store, and analyze vast quantities of information about individuals, Sweden and other Western democracies moved to enact privacy protection legislation.

The second wave arose in the 1980s, when it became apparent that dishonest manipulation of computer functions could cause significant economic loss. Legislatures in advanced industrial societies began to prohibit such behavior as unauthorized access to a computer and as damage to computer data.

As the software and entertainment industries began to recognize the threat posed by unauthorized copying of their products, they persuaded sympathetic governments to expand existing regimes of intellectual property protection. This represented the third wave.

The fourth wave identified by Sieber related to offensive content such as pornography, hate speech, or defamation over the Internet. This wave was very uneven, because of the wide variation across nations in the type of conduct that they find sufficiently objectionable to proscribe by law. Even in regard to child pornography, the type of content where there is the greatest agreement regarding prohibition, legislation differs regarding the definition of a child; the definition of pornography; and whether a "virtual" image that has been digitally created (rather than depicting an actual human subject) should be illegal.

The fifth wave of computer crime legislation involved the law of criminal procedure. This tended to focus on methods for searching and seizing electronically stored evidence, and the responsibilities of telecommunications carriers and service providers to assist law enforcement. The development of computer networks brought new challenges in terms of the appropriate measures for the conduct of searches in networked environments that might extend across jurisdictional boundaries.

A sixth wave of legislation relates to security law, specifically the law relating to surveillance, search, and seizure in the shadow of terrorism. The USA PATRIOT ACT (Public Law 107-56), with its provisions for expanded powers of telecommunications interception, is a prominent example. Subsequent disclosures relating to the authorized (and unauthorized) activities of the National Security Agency have also been noted (Bamford 2008; Greenwald 2014).

The digital age is a moveable feast, however. Cybercrime and efforts to control it will undoubtedly continue to evolve. This will primarily entail further developments in one or more of the "waves" observed earlier. In 2003, for example, unsolicited commercial e-mail, colloquially termed "spam," became an increasingly troublesome issue. A number of jurisdictions sought to respond to the problem by prohibiting the sending of such communications (McCusker 2005). Nevertheless, by 2012 it was estimated that spam comprised approximately 70 percent of all e-mail traffic (UNODC 2013). More recently, the matter of cyberbullying has elicited considerable legislative response (Benzmiller 2013; Citron, 2014). The basic issues, those of content regulation, threats of harm, and their potential conflict with freedom of speech, are ones with which authorities are already familiar.

It is all but certain that the continued diversification of cybercrime will lead to new legal responses (or at the least the continuing modification of old ones) and to new challenges. The key is to develop legislation that will control undesirable conduct while allowing legitimate political expression, commercial activity, and social life to flourish. Unfortunately, this is more easily said than done.

[3]

A TYPOLOGY OF COMPUTER CRIME

Computer crimes come in a variety of forms, and there is no standard way of categorizing them. As we will see, a single computer crime may actually entail a number of distinct offences. And some categories comprise a diverse range of activities.

One approach is to differentiate those crimes in which the computer is

- the *instrument* used to commit the offence;
- the *target* of the offence; or
- *incidental* to the offence (Smith, Grabosky, and Urbas 2004).

This is a useful, if imperfect categorization. As will soon become apparent, the distinction between offences where computers are *instruments* and those where computers are *targets* can involve a great deal of overlap.

Another means of categorizing computer crime is to differentiate between "old" or conventional crimes that are committed with new technology, and "new" crimes that are committed with new technology. Extortion, that is, demanding something of value accompanied by a threat of harm in the event of noncompliance, is an ancient practice. Today, however, extortion threats can be communicated electronically over long distances, and extortion payments made by means of electronic funds transfer (Grabosky, Smith, and Dempsey 2001, ch. 3; Perlroth and Wortham 2014).

Similarly, the production and dissemination of illicit images of children predated the advent of conventional photography. It remained labor intensive until the digital age, when technology enabled instantaneous creation, reproduction, and dissemination of images without having to worry about film development and hand-to-hand transfer (Grant, David, and Grabosky 2001).

Stalking is also an old crime. The offences of watching and besetting, and criminal harassment date back at least to the rise of the trade union movement when striking workers were prevented from behaving in a menacing manner toward strikebreakers. Similarly, bullying existed long before social media. Today, digital technology enables the transmission of persistent, unwanted, harassing communications of whatever kind from the comfort of one's home.

"New" crimes committed with novel technologies tend to involve unauthorized access to, and interference with, information systems. The most dramatic manifestations include denial of service attacks and the dissemination of "worms" and "viruses," collectively known as malicious code. Before considering these crimes, let us first turn our attention to the point at which many different kinds of computer offences begin: hacking.

HACKING

The term "hacking" refers generally to the unauthorized access to a computer or a computer system. For some, this is an end in itself. For others, it is the predicate to more serious offending; many of the offences described next begin with a hack. Most computer systems require some kind of password or access code in order to log on. This can sometimes be determined by guesswork. Some people use their own name or nickname; the term "guest" or "visitor" is not uncommon. Some products come with a standard default password that users do not bother to change. Other hackers obtain passwords through physical investigation. A password might be written on a "post-it" sticker affixed to a person's computer monitor. Alternatively, access information may be obtained through inspection of trash (colloquially referred to as "dumpster diving"). A password may also be obtained by taking the owner of a password into one's confidence and persuading them to disclose it (sometimes called "social engineering"). Automated hacker tools, such as password-guessing programs and other software that probes for vulnerabilities that may allow for remote access to a computer, are readily available on the World Wide Web.

In the days before the takeoff of electronic commerce, when businesses, universities, and governments were less reliant on information technology, hacking was regarded with a degree of tolerance. Law enforcement agencies were not always interested in those very few cases that were drawn to their attention. One of the more celebrated early examples of hacking was described in a book entitled *The Cuckoo's Egg* by Clifford Stoll (1989). Stoll, an astronomer at Lawrence Berkeley Laboratories, was asked to rectify a small anomaly in the accounts of the lab's computer center. He soon discovered that someone had gained unauthorized access to the lab's computer system and was using this to gain further unauthorized access to other systems around the country. Stoll's book relates one of the first (and best) detective stories in the annals of cybercrime, and the entire story is too good merely to summarize here. A firsthand reading of the book is essential.

As the vulnerability of information systems and the institutions dependent upon them became increasingly apparent, hackers began to achieve wider recognition for their technical exploits. Regarded by some as harmless mischief makers and by others as a serious criminal threat, hackers began to achieve a kind of celebrity status. Many thrived on notoriety and adopted flamboyant nicknames or "handles" by which they identified themselves. A twenty-one-year-old university student in Argentina, Julio Cesar Ardita, obtained access to a system at Harvard University and used it to break into the system of the US Naval Command, Control, and Ocean Surveillance Center (NCCOSC). He then installed "sniffer" programs to capture the identification details and passwords of legitimate users. He went on to penetrate a number of other government, educational, and commercial computer systems, including NASA's Jet Propulsion Laboratory in Pasadena, California, and the Los Alamos National Laboratory in New Mexico. Ardita called himself "Griton" ("Screamer" in Spanish) (Goldstone and Shave 1998). Later in this chapter we will see how a fifteen-year-old boy with the handle "Mafia Boy" interrupted the services of major electronic retailers in February 2000.

In 1994, two young hackers in Britain who called themselves "Datastream Cowboy" and "Kuji" broke into a system at a US Air Force base in upstate New York, copied sensitive files, and installed password-sniffing devices. They launched further intrusions into other defense systems around the United States and downloaded large amounts of data. These activities were taken seriously by authorities in the United States

KEVIN MITNICK

One of the more prominent of the early computer hackers was a Californian named Kevin Mitnick, known for a time by the nick-name "Condor." Regarded by some as a cult hero and by others as a "folk devil," in the 1970s he obtained unauthorized access to tele-phone systems in the Los Angeles area. In 1981, he was arrested for destroying data over a computer network. In 1989, he was con-victed under the Computer Fraud and Abuse Act for theft of soft-ware from the Digital Equipment Corporation. Following his release, he continued offending, his notoriety earning him a place on the FBI's Most Wanted List. After a nationwide search, he was rearrested in 1995 and held without bail. In 1999, at the age of thirty-six, he was sentenced to a total of sixty-eight months in fed-eral prison (including time served), followed by three years of su-pervised release. On January 21, 2000, he was released from prison after serving fifty-nine months and seven days. The conditions of his release were extremely stringent. Mitnick is now the principal of an information security consulting firm. He has been the subject and the author of a number of books on his own activities and on computer security more generally (Goodell 1996; Shimomura and Markoff 1996; Mitnick 2002; Mitnick and Simon 2005, 2011; see also http://www.justice.gov/opa/pr/Pre_96/February95/89.txt .html (accessed July 7, 2015) and http://www.kevinmitnick.com/ index.php (accessed July 7, 2015)).

and Britain, and the two were arrested. Datastream Cowboy was sixteen years old, and Kuji was twenty-one (Power 2000, pp. 66–76).

In addition to targeting the information systems of large institutions, hackers sometimes attack each other. A celebrated case involved the "Masters of Deception" and the "Legion of Doom," who, in addition to competing with each other to defeat corporate security measures, sought to infiltrate their rival's systems (Slatalla and Quittner 1995).

Hacking is facilitated by flaws ("bugs") in computer code, particularly in those aspects of an operating system relating to access and security. In

April 2014, a flaw was discovered in the Open SSL protocol, which provides security between individual computers and websites. The communication back and forth is referred to as "heartbeat," and the flaw became known as "Heartbleed." Exploitation of the Heartbleed flaw provided clandestine access to users' personal and financial details, until the flaw was "patched" (Perlroth 2014). Victims included a large healthcare provider and the Canadian revenue office (Reuters 2014).

ILLEGAL INTERCEPTION OF COMPUTER-MEDIATED COMMUNICATIONS

The old practice of tapping into telephone lines has been eclipsed by new technologies. Today, computer-mediated communications are vulnerable to interception for a variety of purposes. People may be voyeuristic, or they may seek to capture sensitive information such as credit card details. They may be engaged in political or economic espionage against foreign states or business competitors (Nasheri 2005). Or they may be mistrustful of a spouse. The scale and sophistication of such endeavors, especially when practiced by governments, are staggering. Disclosures in 2013 by Edward Snowden about the US National Security Agency's global communications surveillance programs revealed that the private communications of German Chancellor Angela Merkel and Brazilian President Dilma Roussef had been routinely monitored. While such actions may not have been in breach of US law (much activity of questionable legality that is undertaken in furtherance of "national security" can be conducted with impunity), they were certainly prohibited by the laws of Germany and Brazil.

Mobile phone technology has further enhanced criminal opportunities. By 2014, the International Telecommunication Union estimated that there were nearly seven billion mobile cellular subscribers worldwide. In a number of countries, there are more cell phones than there are people (mobiThinking 2014). Cellular phones are vulnerable to hacking for a variety of purposes. A successful cell phone hacker may listen in to telephone conversations. Between 2000 and 2006, the former British tabloid newspaper *News of the World* engaged private investigators to hack into the telephones of politicians and celebrities, including members of the royal family, victims of the 2005 London bombings, and a schoolgirl who had been murdered. The remote interception of private conversations or voice mail messages was made easy by the fact that users often fail to change the default access codes provided by mobile phone service providers. The scandal led to numerous inquiries, to the closure of the newspaper, and to the prosecution and conviction of a number of employees of Rupert Murdoch's media organization, News International (Davies 2014).

It is also possible to enable a cell phone to serve as a "bug" to record background conversations, even when the phone is not in use. Moreover, the convergence of global positioning technology and cellular telephony now enables the identification of the phone's physical location, at least when it is turned on. This is a boon to stalkers and other criminals, and a potential threat to the privacy of ordinary, law-abiding citizens. The upside is that it is also useful to those concerned about the whereabouts of their children or elderly relatives, as well as to law enforcement and security agencies.

The colloquial term for technologies that permit the monitoring of someone else's computer is "spyware." For example, a commercially available program called "loverspy" was concealed within electronic greeting cards. When a recipient opened the card, the program secretly installed itself on his or her computer. This enabled the sender to observe all activities on the recipient's computer, including all keystrokes, all incoming and outgoing e-mails, and all websites visited. It was alleged that this technology was acquired by at least 1,000 individuals and used against over 2,000 victims (US Department of Justice 2005a).

ILLICIT MARKETS

As most users of eBay will attest, the Internet and World Wide Web provide an ideal infrastructure for the exchange of goods and services. Unfortunately, digital technology also facilitates illicit online commerce. Among the first illicit online markets were those which enabled the buying and selling of stolen credit card details. The more prominent of these were ShadowCrew, CarderPlanet, and DarkMarket (Glenny 2011). The world of commerce soon expanded to include technologies for skimming and counterfeiting credit cards, malicious software such as viruses and worms (malware), and robot networks (botnets). To avoid the attention of law enforcement, many sites established elaborate processes for vetting of customers, encryption of communications, and the concealment of underground markets. These included Silk Road, which, prior to its closure in October 2013, provided an encrypted Internet forum for the purchase and sale of illegal drugs and other illicit products such as firearms, stolen credit cards, counterfeit currency, forged passports and IDs, and computer-hacking services, as well as murder for hire (Goldstein 2013).

THEFT OF SERVICES

Those unable or unwilling to pay for telephone or Internet services may acquire these services illegally. By gaining unauthorized access to a telephone switchboard or Internet service provider (ISP) account, they may then use them for everyday purposes or on-sell these services for a tidy profit. They may also use them to commit a subsequent crime, much as a bank robber will use a stolen car for a quick getaway.

There are a variety of ways to access services for purposes of theft (Grabosky et al. 2001, ch. 5). The original "phone phreakers" were able to reproduce the 2,600-cycle tone then used in the US long-distance telephone system. Hardware devices, originally referred to as "blue boxes," replicated long-distance tones and enabled the user to bypass the normal telephone switching process. It was discovered that the toy whistles routinely enclosed in packages of a breakfast cereal popular at the time produced this very same tone. The person credited with this insight was henceforth known by the cereal's name, *Cap'n Crunch*. Not long thereafter, the advent of the Internet enabled aficionados of the telephone system to compare notes through such media as *Phrack* and *2600: The Hacker Quarterly*.[1] A low-tech alternative to "phreaking" was adopted by those who misrepresented their identity and then subscribed for a service without paying for it. The most extreme "bad debt" customers run up a big bill and then simply disappear.

Internet services are also vulnerable to theft. In 1995, a twenty-year-old Yale student with the online nickname of "Happy Hardcore" designed a software program that enabled unlimited free access to AOL by exploiting a weakness in the provider's billing system. He was eventually charged and convicted in what appears to have been the first successful prosecution for theft of services from an Internet service provider (Hilzenrath,1997).

One major conspiracy involved a hacker group known as the "Phone Masters," who in the late 1990s hacked into computer systems belonging to major telephone service providers in the United States and stole long-distance calling card numbers. In 1999, two of the principals were convicted and sentenced to forty-one months and two years of imprisonment, respectively, and each ordered to pay $10,000 restitution to the victim corporations, including Sprint, Southwestern Bell, and GTE. According to the Communications Fraud Control Association, the hacking of PABX systems led to losses of $4.42 billion in 2013 (CFCA 2013).

THEFT OF DATA

The kinds of data that might be attractive to a thief can vary widely, from trade secrets, to classified military information, to almost any information that can be on-sold. Commercial organizations place great value on their mailing lists, and large databases of potential customers' contact details can be worth a great deal of money. An employee of a Florida company engaged in the electronic distribution of advertising material obtained unauthorized access to the database of a company that maintains commercial mailing lists and stole over a billion records (US Department of Justice 2005b). Thefts of data for purposes of subsequent public disclosure and theft of intellectual property, from software, to entertainment, to industrial designs, are discussed later.

Theft of Credit Card Details

For obvious reasons, one form of data that is particularly valuable is valid credit card details. Most legitimate e-retailers who accept credit card payment for goods and services go to extraordinary lengths to ensure that the credit card details are secure, and they put in place elaborate systems, including sophisticated encryption systems, to this end. But not all are so cautious; the advent of wireless technology provided a new opportunity to steal credit card details. In late 2003, three men sitting in a car in the parking lot of a large retail store in Michigan gained access to the store's wireless network. The practice was known as "war driving." From there, they accessed the chain's central computer system and the systems of its branches around the United States. They then attempted to install a computer program on the systems of several branch stores to capture the credit card details of local customers. The principal member of the conspiracy entered a plea of guilty and was sentenced to nine years of imprisonment. At the time, this was a record for the longest sentence imposed in a US Federal court for a hacking offence; the most serious online child pornography offences have attracted longer terms (US Department of Justice 2004c).

In 2013, a number of major US retailers came under online attack, apparently from a group of hackers in Eastern Europe. On December 12, the US Department of Justice notified one of the retailers, Target, of suspicious activity involving its payment cards. Forty million customers of the chain were affected and their cards were compromised. The retailer later disclosed that personal data of as many as seventy million customers had also been stolen. News of the attack had a significant adverse effect on the company's sales, and the cost of repairing the breach was significant. All debit cards had to be reissued, and the company reported a decline of 45 percent of profits from the same three-month period of the previous year. Beyond this, the cost of switching to a more secure technology was estimated at $100 million. Soon thereafter, the company's chief technology officer and its chairman and CEO both resigned (Harris 2014).

Espionage

Espionage has been referred to as the world's second oldest profession. The capacity of states to acquire information closely held by friend and foe alike has increased dramatically in recent years, thanks in great part to the application of digital technology. One of the earliest examples of digital espionage was the work of Markus Hess, who was engaged back in the 1980s by the Soviet KGB to hack into defense computer systems in the United States. Many individuals around the world have followed in his footsteps; some have been inquisitive teenagers, but others have been members of, or civilians engaged by, other states' security services.

States also engage in economic or industrial espionage, perhaps not surprising given the relationship between economic well-being and national security. In February 2013, Mandiant, an information security company based in the United States, reported that the Chinese People's Liberation Army (PLA) Unit 61398 was engaged in a large-scale program of economic espionage against foreign businesses (Mandiant Intelligence Center 2013; Sanger, Barboza, and Perlroth 2013). Based in Shanghai, this organization is alleged to have acquired a massive volume of data from a wide variety of industries in English-speaking countries. Information alleged to have been taken includes technical specifications, negotiation strategies, pricing documents, and other proprietary data. In May 2014, the US Department of Justice issued indictments against five men from the PLA alleging a number of offences, including conspiracy to commit computer fraud, economic espionage, and theft of trade secrets (Wong 2014). In January 2015, information disclosed by Edward Snowden included a top-secret document revealing that China had obtained substantial amounts of data on the new US stealth jet, the F-35 Lightning II (Feng 2015). Shortly thereafter, China was suspected of obtaining remote access to vast quantities of personal data relating to security clearances for US government employees (Sanger, Perlroth, and Shear 2015).

The Chinese are not alone. It has been reported that US authorities were spying on the Brazilian oil company Petrobras as well as the Chinese telecommunications and Internet company Huawei (Romero 2013; Reuters Canada 2014; Sanger 2014). In February 2015, it was alleged that US and British intelligence services had penetrated the systems of Gemalto, a French-Dutch company that is the world's largest manufacturer of SIM cards. The alleged attack was undertaken ostensibly for the purpose of acquiring encryption codes that would enable the intelligence services to access large amounts of mobile voice and data communications from around the world (Scott 2015).

State surveillance of US citizens and of foreign nationals has also increased dramatically in the digital age (Freedom House 2014). In 2013 Edward Snowden revealed that the US National Security Agency has captured and stored e-mail traffic and retains the capacity to monitor online activity throughout the world. The general outline of these developments had been disclosed five years previously by James Bamford (2008), but the official documents disclosed by Snowden were both explicit and remarkable. The United States hardly has a monopoly on surveillance of its own and of other nations' citizens. Many states, particularly in the Middle East and Asia, restrict access to websites deemed by authorities to be inappropriate. It has been reported that China employs two million people to monitor blogs (and to delete offending content). Chinese authorities have also been able to access citizens' iCloud accounts and to steal or redirect information entered by the user. Vietnam's "opinion shapers" identify dissident citizens on Facebook and report their "abuse" with a view toward having the activists' accounts suspended (BBC 2013; Mozur, Perlroth, and Chen 2014; Global Voices 2014).

In some cases, dissidents can use technologies to circumvent state censorship and surveillance. A significant proportion of youth in Iran use proxy servers and virtual private networks to enable them to access prohibited sites (Virgillito 2014). During the "Arab Spring" protests of 2011 and 2012, Internet and social media usage was observed to increase in many countries of the region.

Arguably no less sinister is the use of digital technologies by agents of the state for unlawful domestic purposes. In 2014, a former Director of the (South) Korean Intelligence Service was convicted of directing his agents to disseminate information that was critical of opposition political candidates. It was reported that a secret team of agents posted over a million messages over Twitter and other social media to that end (Choe 2014). In that same year, the Inspector General of the US Central Intelligence Agency found that CIA members had penetrated the computer system of the Senate Intelligence Committee. At the time, the Committee was investigating the use of torture by the CIA during the presidency of George W. Bush (Mazzetti and Hulse 2014).

Nowadays, much information relevant to national security is stored in digital form. The use of digital technology to access and copy such material is familiar practice. This is also the case with confidential commercial information. Trade secrets and economic intelligence are often valuable commodities. The competitive nature of international commerce is such that companies face a significant risk of becoming victims of industrial espionage. Competitors, and at times, foreign governments, might seek to acquire strategic economic intelligence, trade secrets, or intellectual property by illegal means (Nasheri 2005). Indeed, for many nations, corporate intelligence collection may be more important than defense intelligence collection. The distinction between these is not always clear (Sanger 2014).

Piracy

Digital technology facilitates perfect reproduction, and speedy and widespread dissemination, of text, images, video, sound, and multimedia combinations. In the early days of the digital age, there were those who claimed that cyberspace was fundamentally different from terrestrial space, and that all information should be free (Barlow 1996). This view was not universally shared, least of all by the software and entertainment industries, whose future depended significantly on the commercialization of digital products. Despite the extension of copyright protection to content that exists in digital form, there were those who sought to copy and distribute intellectual property free of charge, almost as an act of rebellion. More recently, as professional and amateur criminals became aware that there was a great deal of money to be made in pirated content, piracy too became commercialized. Even the file-sharing site The Pirate Bay sold advertising.

An illegal digital piracy group called DrinkOrDie comprised members in a number of countries around the world. They were estimated to have distributed more than $50 million in illegally produced software in the three years prior to their disruption by an investigation culminating in simultaneous raids in a number of countries in December 2001 (Urbas 2006b). Since then, the rapid growth of file-sharing networks and services such as Gnutella, Bitorrent, and Megaupload has further encouraged the dissemination of copyrighted content. Despite the concerted efforts of the software and entertainment industries to enlist (or require) the assistance of Internet service providers (Tusikov 2015), pirated content abounds in cyberspace.

FRAUD

The offence of fraud involves obtaining something of value by means of deception. As such, it is as old as human history. But digital technology has enabled old forms of fraud to be perpetrated with much greater efficiency. One of the most common forms of fraud, discussed later, is called "advance fee fraud," "Nigerian advance fee fraud," or "419 fraud." Many of these frauds have originated in Nigeria, and 419 is the section of the Nigerian criminal code that applies to this type of offence.

One variation is called "romance fraud," as it plays upon the weaknesses of lonely individuals. Victims may be contacted "cold," or approached on online dating sites, by someone purporting to be an attractive stranger seeking to establish a romantic relationship. If the victim responds positively, the stranger then strings the victim along, repeatedly requesting gifts and money, until the victim recognizes that he or she has been deceived. This can endure for a substantial period of time, depending upon the skill of the fraudster and the gullibility of the victim (Kates 2012). This can result in significant financial loss and more. In 2013, an Australian woman was found dead in South Africa, where she had travelled in order to meet a man she had met through an online dating service. The following year, a twenty-eight-year-old Nigerian man was charged with deception. He allegedly received approximately $100,000 from the woman before her death.

The following two messages are typical of the genre. Both are reproduced *verbatim*, . . . verbatim. They were received at different times, but they share similar turns of phrase. The first message appears to have originated from the office of an elected official from the US State of Oregon (the address in question was legitimate), but it contains an explicit invitation to respond to another individual named "Sarah Charles."

From: Sen Steiner Hayward [mailto:sen.elizabethsteinerhayward@state.or.us]
Sent: Saturday, 13 October 2012 1:08 AM
Subject: Hello, please reply to sarahc1147@live.com

Hi,

How are you doing over there? is my pleasure to contact you after coming across your email. I am miss Sarah Charles by name, please I am searching for a good relationship with a real love, pls contact me with my address (sarac1147@live.com) or more introduction also I will send my pictures to you so we can know more about each other. But bear in mind that relationship has no Age, colors barrier, no educational back ground barrier, no social-economic barrier, religious, language, nationality or distance

barrier, the only important thing there is love . . . i promised to answer all
your question through my email . . .
God bless and take care.

Kiss&Hug
Sarah

From: georgeline arisa [mailto:arisa.georgeline23@suomi24.fi]
Sent: Sunday, 2 December 2012 7:48 PM
Subject: Hello Dear From georgeline ,

Hello Dear From georgeline,
how are you today, i hope your doing fine over there. my name is miss
georgeline and i am single. I come across your profile today at and its my
pleasure and interesting sending mail to you as a new friend. and I will like
you to contact me back with my e-mail address , so i can give you my picture and tell you more about me. Remember good relationship goes
beyond distance and color, honest, emotions, careering and kind that lead
both lovers to fly highly on the wings of happiness.
Awaiting to hear from you soon.
Have a nice day.

Yours georgeline

eorgeline.arisa4@hotmail.com

Most readers would regard the following message as too good to be true:

From: Mrs. Ellen Heuman [mailto:heumane@gmail.com]
Sent: Sunday, 16 September 2012 3:53 AM
To: Peter Grabosky
Subject: Re:
Importance: High

Dearly Beloved,
My name is Ellen Heuman a dying woman who has decided to donate
what i have to you/church. I am 69 years old; I was diagnosed with esoph-
ageal cancer 2 years after the death of my husband who has left me

everything he owned. My doctors told me i will not live long because of my health, that is why i decided to WILL/donate my money to you for the good work of humanity, to help the motherless, less privilege and also for the assistance of the widows.

Here are the Contact details of my lawyer:
Name: Tony De Boer
Email: ondboer @aim.com

I have notified him about you. I know i don't know you but i have been directed to do this. I wish you all the best and may the good lord bless you abundantly, and please use the money well and always remember to extend the good work to others.

Yours in the Lord,
Ellen Heuman

A SUSPECT SOLICITATION

(An e-mail message received by the author on December 20, 2005; readers will note the antispam and fraud alert features of the recipient's e-mail system.)
-Originating-IP: [80.89.177.29]
X-Originating-Email: [chies_2005@hotmail.com]
X-Sender: chies_2005@hotmail.com
Reply-To: chiefmrs_odj@yahoo.com
From: "chiea stell" <chies_2005@hotmail.com>
Bcc:
Subject: Urgent Reply
Date: Tue, 20 Dec 2005 09:07:08 -0500
X-OriginalArrivalTime: 20   Dec   2005   14:07:08.0721   (UTC)
FILETIME=[AA3B9210:01C6056E]
X-PMX-Version: 4.7.1.128075, Antispam-Engine: 2.1.0.0, Antispam-Data: 2005.12.20.9 external
X-PerlMx-Spam:Gauge=XXXIIIIIII,Probability=37%,Report='FRAUD_419_X3 1.667, FRAUD_419_X4 1.667, LINES_OF_YELLING_3 0.671, __CT 0, __CT_TEXT_PLAIN 0, __FRAUD_419_LOC 0, __FRAUD_419_MONEY 0, __FRAUD_419_REPLY 0, __FRAUD_

419_TINHORN 0, __HAS_MSGID 0, __LINES_OF_YELLING 0,
__MIME_TEXT_ONLY 0, __MIME_VERSION 0, __RCVD_BY_
HOTMAIL 0, __SANE_MSGID 0, __STOCK_PHRASE_7 0'
X-Spam-Score: * (5)
X-PMX-Spam-Score: # (37%)

OFFICE OF THE CHIEF ACCOUNTANT.
STELLA OBASANJOY FOUNDATION
7, ASUKORO LAGOS NIGERIA

Attention: Sir/Madam,

With due respect, I am Dr. Praise David, the chief accountant to the Nigerian late First Lady, CHIEF MRS. STELLA OBASANJO who died on
Sunday 4th October 2005. Just before her death, the sum of US$30Million
was mapped out meant for Multi-national Hotel Business abroad. For
more details about the first lady visit

http://www.cnn.com/2005/WORLD/africa/10/23/obasanjo.obituary/.

With the help of her only beloved son MUYIWA OBASANJO & the
Board of Trustees, we are genuinely looking for trusted foreigner who
will assist us to establish this Multi-national Hotel Business abroad.
The Hotel will be named after the first lady CHIEF MRS. STELLA
OBASANJO

(memorial)

BENEFITS:

1. THE FOREIGNER WILL BE A SHARE HOLDER OF 15%
   OF TOTAL   EARNINGS.
2. THE FOREIGNER WILL BE THE COMPANY'S REPRE-
   SENTATIVE ABROAD.
3. THE FOREIGNER IS ENTITLED TO ANY BONUS
   FROM THE COMPANY.

Regards

Dr Praise David
God Bless you.

(The recipient did not reply. An expression of interest would most likely have elicited a request for a "facilitation fee" or for the recipient's bank account details and access codes.)

One's immediate reaction to these overtures tends to be one of incredulity. But it should be borne in mind that the fraudsters are not targeting worldly college students (or their professors). Rather, they are seeking to attract just a few hapless souls of limited sophistication and intelligence who may be among the many thousands of recipients. Occasionally, those "hapless souls" will include a few lawyers!

Sales and Investment Fraud

As digital technology permits immediate communications with millions of people at little or no cost, it is ideally suited to advertising goods and services, and to the solicitation of investments. Digital technology has been a boon to legitimate commerce, providing information in unprecedented quantities to inform markets rapidly and efficiently. But it has also been a boon to crooks and con artists.

Fraudulent investment solicitations have been devised for schemes as diverse and bizarre as coconut farming and eel husbandry (Grabosky et al. 2001, pp. 88–90). One of the biggest Internet frauds uncovered to date involved six defendants who were convicted of marketing a scheme over the Internet that defrauded some 172 investors of a total of more than $16 million. Victims were offered an opportunity to "lease" $1 million from a European bank upon payment of a $35,000 fee. They were assured that the "leased" funds would be invested and would generate a return of $5 million over a ten-month period. The scheme was entirely fictitious. The two architects of the scheme were sentenced to sixteen years and eight months, and eleven years and three months of imprisonment, respectively, and ordered to pay restitution of $16,762,000 (US Department of Justice 2002a).

Fraudulent Ordering of Goods

With access to stolen credit card details, or armed with other skills, it is easy enough to order a product online, have it delivered to a temporary address, and then to make off with the goods without actually paying for them. One of the more ambitious examples of such a crime involved the alleged activities of a Romanian hacker who gained access to a computer manufacturer's online ordering system and placed orders for a variety of computers and related equipment, and then instructed that they be shipped to confederates at "mail drops" around the United States. It was alleged that the hacker, who had defeated the company's security safeguards, ordered more than $10 million worth of equipment. He and his confederates had recruited additional individuals, including high school students, to receive the merchandise and then to either sell it and send the proceeds to Romania or repackage the goods and ship them there (US Department of Justice 2004a).

Sharemarket Manipulation

The Internet has dramatically increased the capacity to spread false rumors about shares traded on stock exchanges. Whether through mass e-mailings or through comments made in Internet chat rooms, rumor, hype, or other forms of misinformation can influence the price of shares. By timing one's buy or sell orders carefully, a criminal investor can make a killing, figuratively speaking.

The advent of day trading, where individuals are able to make their own trades rather than use the services of a stockbroker, has made it possible to engineer a pattern of transactions that give the impression of movement in a share price. This can be done by a single person trading on a number of accounts or by two or more individuals acting in concert. In one celebrated case, a fifteen-year-old New Jersey student purchased stock in thinly traded companies and, using "multiple fictitious names," posted numerous messages on finance message boards recommending the purchase of these particular stocks. The messages included predictions that stock was about to "take off," would be the "next stock to gain 1,000%," and was "the most undervalued stock ever." After the prices increased, the youth sold his shares at a profit (US Securities and Exchange Commission 2000).

Auction Fraud

The advent of online auctions was accompanied by a variety of deceptive conduct on the part of both buyers and sellers. In some cases, sellers received payment but failed to deliver the goods or delivered inferior substitutes. In others, buyers would take possession of the goods but fail to pay for them. Another common form of auction fraud is to engineer a number of fictitious bids in order to drive up the price of the item on sale. In one case, three defendants who had offered a number of paintings for sale created more than forty fictitious user IDs on eBay using false registration data and then placed a number of fraudulent bids for the purchase of paintings, significantly inflating the eventual sale price (Bailey 2001).

CYBERCRIME TERMS

Distributed Denial of Service Attack (DDOS): An individual (usually a hacker) gains remote access to a number of computers and directs them against a target (usually a computer system belonging to a government or large commercial entity). By overloading the target computer, the attack will impede legitimate access and may render the system inoperable.

Hacking: Obtaining unauthorized access to a computer.

Malware: Malicious software, including viruses, worms, and other hacker tools.

Pharming: An attack that diverts incoming traffic from a legitimate website to another, counterfeit site, usually for purposes similar to those of phishing.

Phishing: Transmitting a form of spam containing links to Web pages that are designed to appear to be legitimate commercial sites. They seek to fool users into submitting personal, financial, or password data. Clicking on the link may also lead to infection of one's computer by a virus, or it may allow access to one's computer by a hacker (Krone 2005a).

Spam: Unsolicited electronic mail, often transmitted in a large volume, whether for legitimate commercial purposes or in furtherance of fraud.

Spear Phishing: Sending an e-mail message purporting to be from an acquaintance or associate, to deceive the recipient into disclosing private data.

Spim: Messaging spam, directed at users of instant messaging services.

Spit: (Spam over Internet telephony) Unsolicited messages transmitted in bulk through voiceover internet protocols to phones with Internet connections.

Virus: A computer program that may spread from computer to computer, as files containing the program are opened, using up available memory and degrading the "infected" systems and their networked computers.

Worm: A computer program that reproduces itself and spreads through a network, using up available memory. It differs from a virus in that it does not require human intervention (such as the opening of a file) in order to spread.

Unauthorized Funds Transfer

Today, the electronic transfer of funds is common practice in advanced industrial societies. It is not surprising, therefore, that criminals might seek to divert the legitimate transfer of funds or to engineer the transfer of funds from legitimate accounts for their own criminal enrichment. In 1994, a mathematician named Vladimir Levin obtained unauthorized access to Citibank's computer system from his office computer in St Petersburg, Russia. He arranged for accomplices to open bank accounts in Israel, Finland, and California, and then began to transfer funds from legitimate Citibank account holders into the accounts of his co-conspirators (Power 2000, pp. 92–102). As we will see later, similar offences on a much larger scale have occurred more recently.

Embezzlement

Stealing from the boss is as old as the employment relationship. Bosses can steal from companies (and employees), too, as they have since companies were first created. What was once achievable and concealable by means of fancy bookkeeping can now be accomplished with information systems. One employee of a not-for- profit operator of hospitals and clinics in Northern California used her computer to obtain access the company's accounting software. She then issued over one hundred checks to herself and others, resulting in losses of over $875,000.[2]

ATM Fraud

Automatic teller machines are common features in most cities and towns of the industrialized world. While some offenders use brute force (such as ram-raids with motor vehicles) to defeat ATMs, others use more subtle means. Some offenders have constructed dummy ATMs that record a customer's card and PIN details before indicating that the system is out of order. The details are then available for the manufacture of a counterfeit card, and its criminal use on some subsequent occasion, whether at a legitimate ATM or for the purchase of goods and services. Rosoff et al (1998, p. 374) describe how two ex-convicts built a homemade ATM, installed it in a shopping mall, and left it there for over two weeks while it collected credit card details. Unobtrusive attachments to legitimate ATMs include cameras, card swipe readers, and transmitters that enable offenders to remotely capture credit card and PIN numbers. As we have already seen, a thriving market exists for stolen credit card and password data.

Beginning in 2012, an international consortium of cybercriminals used sophisticated intrusion techniques to hack into financial institutions and obtain prepaid debit card data of the banks' cardholders. They then removed withdrawal limits on the cards and sent the details to accomplices positioned in a number of countries, who encoded magnetic stripe cards for use in ATMs. In a matter of hours on December 22, 2012, the group executed more than 4,500 ATM withdrawals in twenty countries and collected about $5 million. Over a period of ten hours on February 19 and 20, 2013, accomplices in twenty-six countries made approximately 36,000 transactions, withdrawing some $40 million (US Department of Justice 2013).

Forgery

Scanning technology has become so refined that perfect copies of documents can be easily made. These can range from identity documents such as birth certificates to currency. Designer labels can also be copied with uncanny accuracy. Image-editing software is widely available, all but permitting one to transform a representation of a sow's ear into that of a silk purse.[3] Websites can also be counterfeit or "spoofed," with uncanny accuracy for a variety of purposes, including fraud and protest.

In 2013, an environmental activist fabricated a press release using the letterhead of a major Australian bank. The document, which was widely transmitted to media organizations, stated that the bank had withdrawn funding to a large coal mining project. Before the hoax was detected and trading suspended, shares in the mining company fell by 6 percent, with the company's value declining by $300 million. The shares recovered their value once the incident was verified as a hoax (Hall 2014).

Some forgeries are less than perfect, however. One aspiring forger who sought to reproduce currency at home using a basic scanner and Page Maker software was convicted of counterfeiting (*United States v. Godman* 223 F.3d 320 [6th Cir 2000]).

DESTROYING OR DAMAGING DATA

There are many ways in which data may be destroyed or damaged. It can be erased or deleted, and it may not be recoverable. It may be encrypted and thereby made inaccessible to anyone without access to the mathematical formula (or encryption key) by which it was transformed. It may be altered in such a manner that diminishes its value or usefulness.

In 2003, the disgruntled former employee of a large Massachusetts high-technology company logged into the company's server and deleted the source code for the software that he had been working on before his contract was terminated. He sought to cover his tracks by altering the computer logs on the server and by impeding access by legitimate employees who were in a position to survey and rectify the damage. Fortunately for the company, the deleted files had been backed up, and the lost data could be retrieved (US Department of Justice 2004b). In August 2012, a cyberattack against Saudi Aramco, the Saudi national oil company, destroyed data held in tens of thousands of computers (Sanger 2015).

The 2014 attack on Sony Pictures, apparently originating in North Korea, resulted in the erasure of a considerable volume of data from the company's servers.

Website Defacement

With the advent of the World Wide Web in the mid-1990s, website defacement became a popular pastime of hackers. It remains so to this day. In 1996, a Swedish hacker group succeeded in altering the website of the CIA so that it read "Welcome to the Central Stupidity Agency" (Neumann 1996). Indeed, this and many other examples of hacked websites are archived on the Web.[4] More recently, as noted later, the terrorist group ISIS succeeded in compromising the Twitter account of the US Central Command, replacing the account's official content with threatening messages.

UNAUTHORIZED PUBLIC DISCLOSURES

In recent years, digital technology has been used to copy and publish confidential national security information. In 2010, Bradley (now Chelsea) Manning, a US Army intelligence analyst, released 250,000 US diplomatic cables and 500,000 army field reports to Wikileaks (Greenberg 2012). In 2013 she was convicted and sentenced to thirty-five years of imprisonment. As we have just seen, Edward Snowden, a former contract employee of the National Security Agency, disclosed thousands of classified documents relating to the NSA's global telecommunications surveillance program. A number of the disclosures contained evidence of questionable behavior on the part of the US Government (Greenwald 2014).

State secrets are not the only kind of information vulnerable to unauthorized disclosure. Intimate personal details, particularly of celebrities or other well-known individuals, are grist for the mill of cyberpaparazzi. These may take the form of intimate words, images, or video that may have been digitally recorded or copied and are easily disseminated to a wide audience. In September 2014 nude images of actress Jennifer Lawrence and others were posted on the online message boards 4chan and Reddit (Isaac 2014). Lesser known individuals too may suffer from unwanted digital exposure. The near ubiquity of digital photography creates boundless opportunities for what is called "revenge pornography," the graphic exposure of a former intimate partner (Citron 2014). Private intimate content may also be used as an instrument of extortion.

Public disclosure of corporate secrets (as opposed to their clandestine, private use to gain a competitive edge) is also an emerging issue. Data may be disclosed in order to call attention to the possibility of illegal conduct on the part of a corporation or its clients. Data stolen from a Swiss subsidiary of HSBC triggered investigations of alleged money laundering by the bank and tax evasion by a number of its clients (Bray 2015). Disclosure may also be made for political purposes or for revenge. In November 2014, a great deal of information from Sony Pictures Entertainment was extracted from the company's computers and found its way to social media. These included employee e-mails (which provided raw material for considerable Hollywood gossip), corporate and individual financial information, Social Security numbers, and scripts of forthcoming productions.

Individuals identifying themselves as "Guardians of Peace" claimed credit for the hack and demanded that the company refrain from releasing a forthcoming motion picture, *The Interview*, a comic depiction of a plan to assassinate North Korean leader Kim Jong Un. The US Government attributed the attack to North Korea, which, despite its expressions of outrage over the disparagement of its leader, denied all responsibility for the hack. Details of the evidence upon which the attribution was based were murky. Initially, it was remarked by US authorities that carelessness on the part of the hackers, and similarity to earlier activity attributed to North Korean agents, revealed their provenance. US authorities subsequently alluded to definitive evidence of North Korean involvement, but they declined to discuss details on national security grounds. It was eventually reported that this evidence was obtained as the result of previous US government penetration and compromise of North Korean networks, which had made them accessible to US agents (Sanger and Fackler 2015).

INTERFERING WITH THE LAWFUL USE OF A COMPUTER

A variety of computer crimes may fall under the general description of "interfering with the lawful use" of a computer. This may or may not entail unauthorized access. The most common tools used in these crimes are worms and viruses, known collectively as "malicious code" or "malware."

In February 2014, a cyberattack degraded the computer systems of Las Vegas Sands, one of the world's largest gambling companies, whose chairman and chief executive is a prominent supporter of Israel. Although the source was not immediately apparent, a year later, the US Director of National Intelligence attributed the attack to Iran (CNN 2015).

TOOLS OF CYBERCRIME

Anonymous E-mail: Concealing information that would identify the originator of a message. (Gordon, Loeb, Lucyshyn, and Richardson 2002).

Botnet (abbreviation of robot network): a system of computers that have been remotely commandeered by a "botmaster," who harnesses the computing power of the captive network to transmit spam or to launch a denial of services attack against a target.

Encryption: The process of mathematically transforming digital information so that it is unintelligible to anyone other than a person in possession of an algorithm or "key" that will permit the data to be converted to its original state.

Key Logger: applications inserted directly on a computer, or installed remotely, that record the user's every keystroke.

Malicious Code: Computer programs designed to allow unauthorized access and/or cause damage to a computer or system; worms or viruses. Also known as "malware."

Man in the Middle Attack: An attack where a third party intervenes in a communication between two individuals, either diverting the communications or altering its content.

Network Scanning Programs: Programs designed to identify networked computers and operating systems that might be vulnerable to attack.

Password Crackers: Programs that generate dictionary words or commonly used passwords that might be used to gain unauthorized access to a computer.

Rootkit: A series of programs that hide evidence of an intrusion or of the existence of a Trojan.

Spoofing: Intentionally misrepresenting sender name and address information to make it appear that a message originated from someone else. URLs can also be used deceptively for parody or fraudulent purposes (http://www.whitehouse.org was not the same as http://www.whitehouse.gov).

Spyware: Technologies that permit clandestine, remote surveillance of a computer, including text, voice, or image. *See also* Key Logger; Man in the Middle Attack.

Steganography: The process of hiding the existence of information (such as text) by concealing it within other information (such as an image).

Trojan Horse: a malicious program disguised as legitimate software but which, when transmitted to an unsuspecting recipient, may impede functioning of the target computer system and may even facilitate unauthorized access to, and control over, that computer, or enable the installation of a key logger.

Malicious Code

The writing of self-replicating computer programs was initially the work of computer systems administrators, diagnosticians, curiosity seekers, and pranksters. In the early days of computing they were of some utility in assessing system performance. Over time, the writing and release of viruses and worms became increasingly the province of the negligent or malicious programmer. Since the mid-1990s, as Internet connectivity has increased in the developed world, the damage that can be inflicted by malicious code has become more apparent. The "I Love You" virus, released from the Philippines in 2000, caused severe degradation of systems around the world. Although a suspect was identified, the absence of a law in the Philippines that criminalized the release of a virus meant that the alleged offender was never brought to trial (Urbas 2006a).

Significant epidemics of malicious code occur with numbing regularity. More recently, the use of malicious code has become more focused. Rather than indiscriminate releases, one sees targeted attacks directed at financial institutions, so-called revenge attacks aimed at personal enemies, and attacks by nation states against adversaries for purposes of espionage or sabotage. Malicious code can also be very useful in the construction of botnets.

Malicious code of a more modest nature appears so frequently that entire industries have developed to detect and remove them. Indeed, any user of a PC who does not have antivirus software installed and regularly updated is at great risk of loss or damage to data.

Denial of Service

For whatever reason, people have sought to shut down, or slow down, computer systems since the earliest days of the digital age. An early strategy for denial of service was a coordinated "blitz" of e-mail messages or website hits against the target computer or system. A large number of users would get together and orchestrate simultaneous activity, which, in sufficient volume, would slow a system down or make it difficult (if not impossible) for legitimate users to obtain access. The colloquial term for this was "mail bombing," a kind of electronic sit-in. During the Kosovo conflict at the end of the 1990s, hackers from Belgrade directed an attack against NATO servers, saturating the system (Denning 2001).

Subsequent developments in technology made denial of service attacks less labor intensive. In what is called a distributed denial of service (DDOS) attack, an individual (usually a hacker) gains remote access to a number of computers and directs them against a target (usually a computer system belonging to a government or large commercial entity). By overloading the target computer, the attack will impede legitimate access and may render the system inoperable. A fifteen-year-old Canadian who called himself "Mafia Boy" did just that in 2000. These techniques have been refined with the use of "botnets" (short for robot networks), computer programs that are controlled by a "botmaster." Some botnets have beneficial uses, but others are employed to gain unauthorized control over a target's computer for for further criminal objectives.

In February 2010, proposals by the Australian Government to introduce a national system of Internet filtering provoked considerable online indignation. Led by the group *Anonymous*, which referred to it as "Operation Titstorm," it entailed denial of service attacks against numerous government websites and defacement of the Prime Minister's website with pornographic images (Moses 2010). The filtering plan was never implemented.

SPAM

The term "spam," taken from an old Monty Python comedy routine, refers generically to unsolicited bulk electronic mail. Spam became a problem, and in many places its dissemination became a crime, around the turn of the twenty-first century when digital technology enabled ordinary individuals to send mass mailings to millions of people at lightning speed, and at a cost of next to nothing. The development of "botnets" allowed purveyors of spam to harness the computing power of others' computer systems, significantly enhancing the volume of unwanted communications. Legitimate or otherwise, unsolicited mass e-mails may cause considerable inconvenience to recipients and may detract from system capacity in any organization. At the extreme, this massive increase in unwanted e-mail traffic detracted from the productivity of large organizations, whose members spent a considerable portion of "company time" disposing of junk e-mail. Alazab and Broadhurst (2014) note that 80 to 90 percent of Internet traffic is spam, and perhaps 20% of that contains, or is linked to, malware.

One disgruntled supporter of the Philadelphia Phillies sent hundreds of thousands of e-mails complaining about the team. He was able to "spoof" or fake the originator's address so that the spam message appeared to come from legitimate newspapers such as the *Philadelphia Inquirer* and *Philadelphia Daily News*. Many of the destination addresses were invalid, causing the automatic "return" of the message to the purported originators, disrupting the e-mail systems of the news organizations in question. The offender was identified with the assistance of an Internet service provider in Canada and was sentenced to four years in prison (US Department of Justice 2005c). In 2009, the investigation of a significant conspiracy to disseminate spam advertising culminated in the conviction of a number of suspects. The accused were alleged to have falsified information used in the transmission of commercial advertising and to have disguised the identities of senders. This was achieved through programs enabling the evasion of antispam filters and other blocking devices and technologies (US Department of Justice 2009).

While the content of some spam is relatively benign, the use of spam to commit more serious criminal activity has become widespread. Among the more common uses of spam are the dissemination of fraudulent investment solicitations, including variations on the classic Nigerian advance fee fraud letter, the purported sale of pharmaceuticals (such as Viagra) without prescription, and "phishing," deceptive requests for personal financial details (see later). The logic of spam for such criminal purposes is economic, much as is the case for its use in legitimate commercial advertising. The likelihood of any one recipient of a fraudulent solicitation responding positively is small. But communications received by a million individuals will inspire some takers. It only takes a few gullible people to make a fraudster's day.

PHISHING

One of the more recent instruments of online crime is "phishing." Alazab and Broadhurst (2014) note that spammers may obtain legitimate e-mail addresses from commercial sources or may "harvest" them from the Internet. They may also conduct a "dictionary attack," a combination of randomly generated usernames with known domain names to guess correct addresses. They may also purchase address lists from other individuals or organizations such as in underground markets. These are all good reasons why one should not respond to, or even open, an e-mail that appears to be from a suspicious sender. One application of spam that has been particularly troubling in recent years is the practice known as "phishing." This most commonly entails the posting of mass e-mails purporting to be from a legitimate source, usually a financial institution. The e-mail message, often embellished with a forgery of the institution's letterhead, or linked to a counterfeit Web page, may say that it is conducting a security audit and would like to verify the user's account number and access code or PIN number. Alternatively, a phishing overture may appear to originate from a trusted source such as a systems administrator. It may even appear to have been sent by an acquaintance or associate; as we saw with the "I Love You" virus, it is possible to compromise an e-mail account and to send messages to individuals listed in the account's address book.

Another variation of phishing entails the inclusion of a website link in the message, with an invitation to access it. Clicking on the link may expose one's computer to a virus or grant access to an intruder who may then use one's computer for a variety of criminal activities.

From: XXX Bank Limited aviolations@xxx.com.au Sent: Wed 26/02/2014 9:14 AM

To:

Cc:

Subject: XXX Terms and Conditions Violation
Important Information Regarding Your XXX Bank Account.

Dear member,
We are writing regarding your XXX Bank Account
Case ID : (29280-292-1200-82991-2)

We have reasons to believe that you have violated our Terms and Conditions. As you had some problems with the Deposit Interest Retention Tax, we have limited access to your XXX Bank account features. We understand
that this may be an inconvenience but please understand that this temporary limitation is your last warning.
Please read again with attention our Terms and Conditions and try to respect them.

SERVICE : XXX Internet Banking.
SERVICE : XXX Credit Card.
EXPIRATION : Wednesday, February 26, 2014

What you need to do - Activate your XXX Bank account :

XXX Bank Account - SUSPENDED - Activate Account

- Update your information immediately.

Thanks,
XXX Bank Terms Violations Department.

———————————————————————

From: Tristan, Sylvia A
Sent: Monday, August 27, 2012 5:29 PM
To: notice@domain.org
Subject: WEBMAIL ADMIN*Quota Limit Exceeded

This Message is From Help-desk.Your Email Quota is exceeded.You are advised to re-validate your account immediately.Failure to this,will result to seizure to sensitive options in your web-mail.

Verify Here <https://docs.google.com/spreadsheet/viewform?formkey= dGw2eGJlVVdxRElsTFdZY2Q3clNMbXc6MQ>

Thank you for your cooperation.

The recipient of the following message had been a permanent resident of Australia for thirty-six years at the time of receipt:

From: Australia Resettlement [mailto:resettlement.aus4@gmail.com]
Sent: Tuesday, 27 January 2015 10:13 AM
Subject: You Have Been Selected for Australia 2015 Family Resettlement.

Department of Immigration
Australia Government
The Forrest Centre 219-221 St Georges Terrace
Perth WA, Australia

Attn. Please

Family Resettlement to Australia.

This is to congratulate you for being selected in 2015 Australia Family Resettlement Program, you are among the list that have been nominated for 2015 resettlement to Australia from our head of mission and we will grant your resettlement and benefits on the condition that you meet some basic requirements.

Every year certain number of people are selected through our electronic ballot system for resettlement by Australia Government as part of support to some Countries.

Please confirm receipt of this notification, by responding immediately. So that we can forward the relevant requirements.

Note: If you receive this notice repeatedly, it is to ensure it delivers safely into your box without failure delivery due to network problem

Contact us email:
resettlement.au@diplomats.com
office.resettlement@diplomats.com

Best Regard,
Australia Resettlement Dept

The notification of an impending "tax refund" may well contain a devious invitation to receive malicious code The tax file number noted in the message is *not* that of the recipient. It is not uncommon to receive messages such as these around tax time:

From: ATO@my.com.au [mailto:ATO@my.com.au]
Sent: Monday, 13 October 2014 11:00 AM
To: Peter Grabosky
Subject: Tax Refund

Dear peter.grabosky@anu.edu.au ,

You are eligible to receive a tax refund of $247.09 according to the last annual calculations of your fiscal activity.

Your tax file number is: 5810283

Please download the tax refund form using the following link
Click here to continue

EXTORTION

Extortion in the "meat world" is as old as human civilization. Let us look more broadly for a moment at the offence of cyber-extortion. By this we mean the use of digital technology to obtain something of value by threatening harm to the victim. Digital technology may be applied to extortion in numerous ways (Grabosky, Smith, and Dempsey 2001, ch. 3).

- The Internet can be used as the medium by which a threat is communicated.
- The victim's information systems may be the target of the extortion threat.
- Where the offence entails blackmail (the threatened disclosure of embarrassing facts about the victim), the Internet may be the medium through which the offensive information is communicated.
- Electronic funds transfer may be used as a means of effecting an extortion payment.
- The Internet and World Wide Web may be used to obtain personal information that may identify or be used against prospective victims.

In recent years, the term "ransomware" has been used to refer to malicious software that infects a target computer and displays a notice containing a threat to encrypt or destroy data unless the user makes a payment. Some ransomware threats are no less fraudulent than they are extortionate. They are presented as communications from law enforcement agencies or information security companies (Perlroth 2012). Imagine the sudden appearance on your screen of a Web page bearing the logos of the US Department of Justice, the Department of Homeland Security, and the Federal Bureau of Investigation, accompanied by the ominous message that "Your computer has been locked!" due to "suspicion of illegal content downloading and distribution." You are then advised that the content in question may entail child pornography, attracting a prison term between four and thirty years and a fine of up to $250,000. You are then advised that your conduct can be deemed to be "occasional/unmotivated" and the matter can be closed without prosecution and your computer unlocked upon electronic payment of $300 through some type of stored value technology, whether bitcoin or a prepaid cash card (Malware Tips 2015). Such anonymous e-payment systems make it easier to collect a payment without revealing one's identity or location.

Variations on this fraudulent overture may entail the opportunity to purchase "security software" to remediate your compromised computer. In the most serious cases, your data may be encrypted, and you are invited to purchase a key that will enable you to recover your data (Geier 2014).

MONEY LAUNDERING

Concealing the proceeds of crime, or concealing legitimately earned income from taxation authorities, is referred to as money laundering. The process involves transforming ill-gotten gains ("dirty money") into funds from an apparently legitimate source ("clean money"). Electronic financial transactions are, in principle, traceable. However, the ability to transfer funds around the world, at the speed of light, through accounts in various jurisdictions that may not have the interest in or capacity to trace financial transactions, makes the identification and interdiction of money laundering difficult. Online banking provides new opportunities for masking the origin of funds. By recruiting unwitting accomplices such as students (often through online media) and seeking their assistance (in return for a fee) in transferring funds offshore, a money launderer may circumvent cash transaction reporting requirements.

The US government has expressed particular concern about the use of online gambling facilities in furtherance of money laundering (Malcolm 2002). Online casinos provide a variety of financial services to their customers, including credit accounts, facilities for the transmittal of funds, and currency exchange services. They may be located in jurisdictions that do not require record keeping or cash transaction reporting. By transferring ill-gotten gains to a casino, gambling a small amount, then obtaining repayment of remaining funds, the apparent source of the funds will be the casino, not the criminal activity that generated the money in the first place.

OFFENSIVE CONTENT

Content of questionable taste, or of unquestionably *bad* taste, abounds in cyberspace. Many countries have made the possession or dissemination of certain kinds of online content criminal offences. Perhaps the most familiar form of illegal content in the United States involves sexual images of children. The People's Republic of China objects to content extolling the virtues of Falun Gong, or of Taiwanese or Tibetan independence. Islamic countries prohibit a wide variety of erotica and do not tolerate content that they regard as insulting to their religion. Many European countries make it a crime to host or to disseminate neo-Nazi propaganda. The United States and some other countries criminalize online gambling.

Almost everyone who has ever accessed the World Wide Web will have encountered, intentionally or otherwise, some offensive content. Digital technology and its recent applications make it easier for anyone to disseminate offensive material. The practice of young people in many countries to create intimately explicit images of one another ("sexting") may well entail violations of the law.

The problem of content regulation is that it is very difficult to censor the Internet, which was designed to withstand damage to one or more components. Content originating on the other side of the world is just as accessible as material hosted on a server next door. Putting a particular site out of commission may work for a while, but sooner or later someone else may come along and start again. Countries may take draconian steps such as insisting that all content be filtered through a government server, but this comes at a price: online access may be more difficult, and legitimate use may be constrained. Countries such as North Korea that actively discourage Internet access by all but a few trusted citizens have placed political control ahead of education and economic development as national priorities. The challenge facing authorities in the People's Republic of China is how to manage the contradictions between the imperatives of a twenty-first-century information society essential to economic development and the perceived need to suppress criticism of the state and its senior officials (Austin 2014).

STALKING AND BULLYING

Stalking is not unique to the digital age. Persistent, unwanted harassing communications are not new. We have already referred to the offence of "watching and besetting." Obscene telephone calls are as old as telephony. But digital technology certainly increases the capacity of those who would like to direct unwelcome communications against a target (Ogilvie 2000). This can be done repeatedly, at the click of a mouse. Moreover, digital technology can be mobilized to recruit others and involve them in activities against the victim.

In one case, a rejected suitor posted invitations on the Internet under the name of a twenty-eight-year-old woman, the would-be object of his affections, saying that she had fantasies of rape and gang rape. He then communicated via e-mail with men who replied to the solicitations and gave out personal information about the woman, including her address, phone number, details of her physical appearance, and how to bypass her home security system. Strange men turned up at her home on six different occasions, and she received many obscene phone calls. While the woman was not physically assaulted, she would not answer the phone, was afraid to leave her home, and lost her job (Miller and Maharaj 1999). One former university student in California used e-mail to harass five female students, apparently in response to their teasing him about his appearance. Using a professor's credit card, he bought information on the Internet about the women and then sent one hundred messages, including death threats, graphic sexual descriptions, and references to their daily activities (Associated Press 1999).

For some years now, developments in digital technology have permitted exploitation of a back door into the operating system of the victim's computer. Offenders have been able to insert Trojan horses or other Spyware in the computers of their targets, enabling them to monitor their victims' keystrokes and even take control of their computer. Digital geolocation technology has also been used to identify the physical location of stalking victims; analysis of geo-tags embedded in digital images may also serve such a purpose (Goodman 2015).

Bullying is greatly facilitated by digital technology (Citron 2014). In 2006, a thirteen-year-old Missouri girl hanged herself after having received humiliating messages on a MySpace account. It was alleged that the messages, which appeared to have been sent by a young boy, were in fact hoax messages sent by the mother of another teenage girl who lived nearby. The defendant was convicted of a misdemeanor charge under the Computer Fraud and Abuse Act, but the conviction was overturned on appeal (Steinhauer 2008).

In addition to lending itself to relentless abuse and harassment, digital technology enables gross violations of privacy and subsequent humiliation. In September 2010, a Rutgers freshman, Tyler Clementi, asked his roommate to vacate their room for a brief period so that he might spend some time alone with a friend. The roommate agreed, but unbeknownst to Clementi, he configured a PC in the room to record the assignation. Clementi and his friend happened to be gay, and the roommate shared the vision of their encounter using a video chat program. Clementi killed himself three days later by jumping from the George Washington Bridge (Foderaro 2010).

CRIMINAL CONSPIRACIES

Just as other communications media such as the telephone have made it easier for collaborating criminals to coordinate their activities, so too has digital technology facilitated communication in furtherance of criminal (including terrorist) conspiracies. Technologies of *encryption* make these communications difficult to access for anyone other than the intended recipient (Denning and Baugh 2000). Encryption entails a process of mathematically transforming digital information (scrambling all those 1's and 0's) so that they are unintelligible to anyone other than a person in possession of an algorithm or "key" that will permit the data to be converted to its original state. A similar technology called *steganography* entails embedding information in an image. What may look like a beautiful mountain landscape may in fact conceal records of illegal drug transactions.

Encryption is both a blessing and a curse. It helps protect privacy from the prying eyes of voyeurs, business competitors, or a repressive government. It provides a modicum of security for legitimate commercial electronic transactions, without which a vibrant online economy cannot flourish. On the other hand, however, encryption provides criminal conspirators with a powerful tool for concealing electronic evidence (Denning and Baugh 2000).

Digital communications between criminals (or between would-be criminals) may also take place in public. Schneider (2003) describes how chemists use Internet Relay Chat and newsgroups to exchange information on the manufacture and distribution of synthetic illicit drugs and their precursor chemicals. The use of text messages to organize collective activity has also become common (Rheingold 2002). Not all of this activity is legal. Australia, for example, has seen the use of text messages to make plans for group sexual assaults and race riots (Morton 2004; *New York Times* 2005). In 2010, riots over increasing prices of food and electricity were organized in Mozambique by SMS (Afronline 2010). New Zealand Police have expressed concern over the use of social media to arrange fights (van Kempen 2014). The group *Anonymous* has coordinated denial of service attacks against diverse targets and, most recently, has threatened to attack the Islamic State.

Today, the widespread use of digital technology in everyday life means that many "ordinary" crimes will involve some aspect of high technology.

Most business records are electronically stored. Cellular phones and personal digital assistants are becoming widespread. Global positioning technology now enables the identification of an individual's movements in time and space. We have reached the stage where many if not most crime scenes will contain some element of digital technology.

The Internet also enables prospective offenders to meet prospective victims. Aside from varieties of fraud discussed later, the most prominent uses of the Internet for such purposes involve adults seeking to meet minors for indecent purposes. Most typically, pedophiles join chat rooms frequented by younger people, develop an electronic relationship, and then arrange to meet somewhere in the physical world. Urbas (2010) describes the case of Toby Studabaker, a thirty-two-year-old former US Marine who befriended a twelve-year-old girl from Manchester, England, in an online chatroom. He arranged to meet her in Manchester. After the girl left home without telling her parents of her plans, the two flew to Paris and then traveled by train to Strasbourg and Stuttgart. When it became apparent that the missing girl had become the subject of an intensive search by European police, she flew home to Manchester and Studabaker turned himself in. He was extradited to the United Kingdom, where he pleaded guilty to charges of abduction and incitement to gross indecency.

New applications of digital technology provide new opportunities for this type of offending. In 2012, three men were accused of raping children whom they had met through a smartphone app (Perlroth 2013).

A more extreme variation on the theme of online offender–victim interface involved a German man, Armin Meiwes, who advertised on the Internet for a person who wanted to be killed and eaten. A fellow German took up the offer. Despite the apparent consent of the victim, the accused was convicted of manslaughter and sentenced to eight-and-a-half years in prison. The government, as German law allows, successfully appealed on the grounds that the sentence was too lenient, and the accused was retried in January 2006. At the second trial, he was convicted of murder and sentenced to life imprisonment (Bernstein 2006).

CYBERWAR AND CYBERTERRORISM

One of the more significant developments regarding cybercrime in the twenty-first century has been the involvement of states (or their proxies) as perpetrators. Such activities entail three different functions: espionage, surveillance, and various forms of damage to an adversary's information systems.

States also engage in activities intended to disrupt computer systems, interfere with the lawful use of these systems, and to damage or destroy data contained within. For obvious reasons, offensive cyberoperations of this kind tend to be shrouded in secrecy. Goodman (2015) notes that the US National Security Agency's British counterpart, the Government Communications Headquarters (GCHQ), has used denial of service attacks to disrupt the activities of the hactivist group, Anonymous. Zetter (2014, p. 198) reports an unsubstantiated suggestion that a 1982 pipeline explosion in Siberia resulted from corrupted software clandestinely positioned in the Soviet supply chain by the CIA. The software controlled pumping equipment on the pipeline and was altered to produce excessive pressure, allegedly producing a three-kiloton explosion. A more recent example of cybersabotage was the joint US/Israeli operation against Iran's nuclear enrichment facilities at Natanz (Sanger 2012, ch. 8; Zetter 2014). As he was about to take office in 2009, President-Elect Obama was advised by his predecessor George W. Bush that the United States and Israel were collaborating in a program to impede the development of nuclear weapons by the Islamic Republic of Iran. The program, which continued under the Obama administration, involved the insertion of very complex malware into the control systems of the Natanz facility. The codename of the operation was *Olympic Games,* and the malware was commonly referred to as "Stuxnet." Centrifuges used in the process of uranium enrichment are very fragile, and by abruptly changing the speed at which the centrifuges operated, the malware succeeded in destroying a significant number of them. The attack was exceptionally sophisticated. The industrial control systems that regulated the enrichment process were compromised, enabling the attackers to disarm alarm systems and to send false indications to technicians in the control room that the systems were operating as normal. This brought about significant delays in the Iranian nuclear development schedule.

The Internet itself was designed under the auspices of the US Department of Defense as a communications system sufficiently robust as to withstand a nuclear attack. Given its pervasiveness, it is not surprising that digital technology has extensive military applications. As the twentieth century drew to a close, weapons systems, defense communications, and logistics all came to depend on software. Predictably, the inescapable reliance on digital technology by both military and civilian institutions has brought about a new dimension in warfare. Not only have military applications become potential targets, but civilian systems have as well. A vast industry has emerged to develop offensive cyber weapons and defensive technologies to protect against them. It has been reported that over one hundred states around the world have, or are developing, offensive cyber capabilities. The United States is but one of these, as *Operation Olympic Games* would suggest; among Edward Snowden's disclosures was a Presidential Policy Directive that, inter alia, directed US officials to draw up a list of foreign targets for potential cyberattack.[5] Presumably, many other governments have invested in offensive cyber operations, as well as in cyber defense (Denning 2014).

Cyberwarfare may also be used as complementary to "on the ground" military operations. Russian military activity on the Crimean Peninsula in 2014 combined cyber and terrestrial activity. Time-tested tactics such as electronic "jamming" and severing communications cables were accompanied by cyberattacks to isolate Ukrainian military forces on the peninsula (Gordon 2014).

The precise organizational auspices of offensive operations are often problematic in cyberspace, as they are in terrestrial space. Aggressive acts, by whatever means, may be undertaken by nonstate actors acting independently (as was the case with the 9/11 attacks) or in collusion with state authorities. The auspices of a cyberattack may be unclear, and precise attribution may be impossible. States may prefer to arrange an attack "at arm's length" for purposes of maintaining plausible deniability. In addition, attacks may be routed through a number of jurisdictions on their way to their target. Attribution remains one of the greatest challenges facing those whose job it is to respond to a cyberattack.

Recent history has seen numerous cyberattacks of uncertain provenance. In 2007, cyberattacks were apparently launched from Russia against government servers in Estonia. The extent of state involvement in these events is unclear; while there appears to be no concrete evidence of direct state activity, it does seem that the Russian government may have implicitly supported or encouraged the attacks (Landler and Markoff 2007; Ashmore 2009). The term "patriotic hackers" has been used to refer to attacks by one country's citizens against a foreign adversary.

There are established principles in international law regarding when and how a state may respond to a cyberattack. An impressive start to the development of such principles may be seen in the Tallinn Rules, recently advanced by an international group of scholars (Schmitt 2013). The key precepts are self-defense, necessity, proportionality, and the minimization of harm to innocent third parties. One should not use force unless it is essential to achieve an objective. If less intrusive means of attaining the objective are available, they should be used. If force must be employed, one should not use more than is required. And steps should be taken to avoid collateral damage. In addition to response in kind (a cybercounterattack), other measures are possible. In April 2015, President Obama authorized the use of financial sanctions against foreign state hackers (Nakashima 2015). It is not inconceivable that conventional armed force might also be considered, depending on the circumstances.

Terrorism

One of the more prominent issues of our time is the threat of terrorism. The term "cyberterrorism" has been used rather loosely to refer to the application of digital technology to terrorist activity. One way of conceptualizing cyberterrorism is Denning's (2000, p. 10): "unlawful attacks against computers, networks and the information stored therein when done to intimidate or coerce a government or its people in furtherance of political or social objectives."

For some years now, thoughtful people in industrialized societies have been alert to the threat of attacks against what we call *critical infrastructure*. In other words, communications, electric power, air traffic control, and financial systems all depend on software and are vulnerable to disruption. The annals of cybercrime contain examples of successful attacks against air traffic control systems, sewage treatment facilities, and large electronic retailers, as well as the occasional disruption of government servers and defacement of government websites. While none of these meet Denning's definition, Hardy (2010) notes that some governments

CRIMINAL ATTACKS ON CRITICAL INFRASTRUCTURE

In March of 1997, a computer hacker disabled a telephone company computer serving the local airport in Worcester, Massachusetts. This disrupted services to the airport's control tower for a period of six hours. The attack also shut down a circuit that enabled aircraft to activate the airport runway lights on approach. NYNEX (later Bell Atlantic) notified the US Secret Service, which shared responsibility for computer crime investigation with a number of federal agencies. Investigations led to a juvenile who had also disrupted local telephone service and had accessed the prescription records of a local pharmacist. The case was the first US Federal prosecution of a juvenile for a computer crime. The youthful suspect pleaded guilty and was sentenced to two years of probation, 250 hours of community service, was required to pay restitution to the telephone company and was prohibited from possessing a modem or other means for remotely accessing a computer or network.[6]

In February 2000, a person obtained remote access to a number of computers at US universities and then directed their computing power against a number of prominent e-commerce sites, including CNN, Yahoo, Amazon.com, eBay, and Dell. The targets were flooded with data, impeding their normal operation. Some were shut down completely; others were seriously degraded to the extent that it took users minutes to access the targets' Web pages. The attacks were of particular concern in that they threatened public confidence in the security of electronic commerce, then in its relatively early stages. It became apparent that the attack had originated in Canada. The Royal Canadian Mounted Police arrested a fifteen-year-old Canadian boy who had boasted of various exploits over the Internet. "Mafia Boy," as he called himself, was sentenced to eight months detention in a youth training center.[7]

In March 2000, a failure at a sewerage pumping station operated by Maroochy Shire in Queensland, Australia, caused the discharge

(continued)

of 264,000 gallons of raw sewage onto the grounds of a five-star resort and nearby parklands. A forty-nine-year-old employee of the company that installed the system, said to have been an unsuccessful applicant for a job with the Shire, was found with a laptop computer, a remote telemetry system, and a two-way radio and antennae. He was alleged to have made at least forty-six attempts to gain control of the system and was sentenced to two years imprisonment *R v Boden* [2002] QCA 164 (01/0324) Davies JA Muir J Wilson 10/05/2002.[8]

On September 20, 2001, computer systems at the Port of Houston, Texas, the eighth largest shipping port in the world, were the target of what appeared to be a denial of service attack. The Port's Web service became unavailable to shipping companies, piloting and mooring services, and others essential to maintaining Port operations. The Port may not have been targeted intentionally, as the attack appears to have been aimed at a chat room user who was perceived to have offended the girlfriend of the alleged perpetrator. The attack traveled through various intermediary computers before reaching the target PC; one of these was at the Port of Houston. The accused, a resident of England, denied any knowledge of the attack, claiming that the evidence was planted on his computer by hackers unknown, who had used a Trojan Horse program. The jury accepted the defense, and the accused was acquitted (Brenner et al. 2004).

may be moving perilously close to defining terrorism broadly enough to embrace lesser forms of political protest.

Although the "electronic Pearl Harbor" scenario may be remote, there are a number of ways in which digital technology may be used in furtherance of, or complementary to, terrorist activity. Digital technology of course may be used for the remote detonation of explosive devices. And while Denning may be correct in asserting that terrorists continue to prefer truck bombs to logic bombs, the use of a cyberattack to complement or enhance a terrestrial attack should not be discounted. Imagine, for example, if an attack on the scale of 9/11 were accompanied by a takedown of the telephone and electric power systems in the target metropolitan area.

Technology as a Means to Facilitate Terrorism

Of course, digital technology can enhance the efficiency of any organization, legitimate or otherwise, that makes use of it. For example, it lends itself nicely to a number of terrorist applications (Thomas 2003). The Islamic State, which rose to prominence in 2014, has engaged in sophisticated use of the Internet and social media for a variety of these (Shane and Hubbard 2014).

Intelligence

Terrorists may seek to acquire open source (publicly available) intelligence on an adversary, or collect classified information by hacking into the adversary's computer systems.

Communications

Members of terrorist groups may send and receive messages, often concealing their content through encryption and steganography (concealing messages within images). The nature of the Internet and World Wide Web is ideally suited to communications across widely dispersed elements of a network. Osama bin Laden, understandably disinclined to go online personally when he became the subject of a manhunt after 2001, used couriers to send communications from internet cafes to his followers around the world.

The use of digital technology in support of tactical terrorist operations has become highly sophisticated. The 2008 siege of Mumbai by Lashkar-e-Taiba (LeT), a Pakistani group affiliated with Al Qaida, represents a chilling example (Goodman 2015, ch. 6). The operation was funded by Filipino affiliates who raised funds by committing online fraud. Insurgents arrived in Mumbai by sea, guided by GPS navigation. They used Google Earth to identify target buildings. Terrorists on the ground in Mumbai verified the identity of one hostage by arranging for an Internet search that yielded his photograph. Commanders of the operation in Pakistan monitored global media coverage of the event and advised their members of tactical developments in the counterterrorist operation. The attack resulted in the death of 166 individuals and injuries to hundreds of others.

Propaganda

Terrorist groups may communicate directly to a general worldwide audience, or to specialist target audiences, bypassing journalistic editing and government censorship. This may include inflammatory hate speech intended to legitimize violence against specified adversaries. The Dudaev brothers, responsible for the Boston bombings in April 2013, were followers of the English language version of the Yemen-based online Al Qaida magazine, *Inspire* (Cooper, Schmidt, and Schmitt 2013). The rise of the Islamic State in 2014 was accompanied by widespread and extremely sophisticated use of the Internet and social media for propaganda purposes (Al Hayat Media 2014). Perhaps the most dramatic example involved the IS commandeering of the US Central Command (CENTCOM) Twitter and YouTube accounts in January 2015 (Cooper 2015; see box).

In 2014, the Somali terrorist group Al-Shabab used Facebook to order a ban on the use of the Internet, and they directed service providers to terminate Internet services within two weeks (Raghavan 2014).

Psychological Warfare

The Internet may be used as a means of tactical deception by terrorist organizations. By generating anomalous patterns of traffic they can give the erroneous impression that an operation may be imminent. The fabrication of "chatter" may distract law enforcement and intelligence services from true terrorist activity.

Another form of psychological warfare can involve general or specific threats or displays of force. Webcasts of hostages, and even hostage executions and bombings, can reach the world.[9] These may be coupled with threats against nationals of specific countries who may be identified with causes that are anathema to the terrorist organization.

Fundraising and Recruitment

Terrorist groups may raise funds through charity and other front organizations, or they may actively seek to recruit new members. Imam Samudra, convicted architect of the 2002 Bali bombings, reportedly called upon his followers to commit credit card fraud in order to finance militant activities (Sipress, 2004). The cities of the world house many young resentful Muslim males, some of whom may well be attracted to militant causes. Webcasts that celebrate martyrdom may be particularly useful in attracting the attention of prospective suicide bombers. The Islamic State appears to have been singularly successful in their online recruitment efforts.

Training

Terrorist groups may use the Internet and the Web for instructional purposes, to teach attack techniques and skills. The surviving 2013 Boston bomber disclosed that he and his brother learned their bomb-making technique online. (Cooper, Schmidt, and Schmitt 2013). Training materials were also found on the computers of alleged terrorists in Sydney, including materials for a book entitled *Provisions on the Rules of Jihad: Short Judicial Rulings and Organisational Instructions for Fighters and Mujahideen Against Infidels* (*Khazaal v. R* (No 2) [2013] NSWCCA 140)[10]. See also *R v Benbrika & Ors* (Ruling No 7) [2007] VSC 425 (30 October 2007)[11].

ISLAMIC STATE VERSUS US CENTRAL COMMAND

The US Central Command, responsible for US military operations in the Middle East, uses Twitter <@CENTCOM> and YouTube <https://www.youtube.com/user/centcom> as platforms for public information. Its Twitter followers number in excess of 100,000.

Typical postings on @CENTCOM entail brief statements such as "U.S. and Coalition forces continued to attack #ISIL terrorists in #Iraq and #Syria Jan. 21-22" followed by a link to the CENTCOM website. A representative CENTCOM YouTube video is entitled "Airstrike against three ISIL warehouses, Dec. 29, near Fallujah, Iraq" <https://www.youtube.com/watch?v=cAHPYtzyysc>

In January 2015, hackers claiming to represent the Islamic State succeeded in gaining control over CENTCOM's Twitter and YouTube accounts, and sent out content that diverged significantly from normal CENTCOM communications. Two IS propaganda videos were posted on the CENTCOM YouTube account. Twitter postings included messages such as "In the name of Allah, the Most

(*continued*)

Gracious, the Most Merciful, the CyberCaliphate continues its CyberJihad." "American soldiers, we are coming, watch your back." "You'll see no mercy infidels. ISIS is already here, we are in your PCs, in each military base. We won't stop! We know everything about you, your wives and children. US soldiers! We're watching you!"

CENTCOM's Twitter and YouTube accounts were temporarily closed, and the offensive content removed. Normal operations resumed within a few hours.

The IS intrusions were regarded as rather embarrassing, especially since they occurred during a week when President Obama was addressing the nation on issues in cybersecurity. The postings went beyond insult, however, when they included the names and addresses of a number of US military personnel (Cooper 2015).

[4]

CYBERCRIME EXPLAINED

To understand where and why cybercrime occurs, it is helpful to rely on a theoretical framework. One useful perspective is that of routine activity theory (Cohen and Felson 1979). Although developed to explain conventional "street" crime, the theory is sufficiently robust to account for cybercrime as well. Essentially, cybercrime can be explained by the intersection of three factors:

1. A supply of motivated offenders
2. The availability of suitable targets or prospective victims
3. The absence of capable guardians

Each of these factors must be present in order for a cybercrime to take place. Remove at least one, and a crime will not occur. Unfortunately, this is usually more difficult than it may appear.

MOTIVATED OFFENDERS

The supply of motivated offenders is in part a reflection of the number of individuals with access to the tools of cybercrime. All else being equal, the more people who are connected to the Internet, the more who are in a position to use the technology for illegal purposes.

To date, in Western industrial societies at least, there has been an exponential growth in the number of people with access to computers. Tables 4.1 and 4.2 illustrate the differential take-up of digital technology around the world. The term "digital divide" refers to the uneven distribution of the uptake and penetration of digital technology. The tables reveal that about 40 percent of people around the world have accessed the

TABLE 4.1 WORLDWIDE INTERNET USERS

	2005	2010	2015
World population (billion)	6.5	6.9	7.3
Not using the Internet	84%	70%	56.6%
Using the Internet	16%	30%	43.4%
Users in the developing world	8%	21%	35.4%
Users in the developed world	51%	67.1%	82.2%

Source: International Telecommunications Union 2015.

TABLE 4.2 INTERNET USERS: PERCENTAGE OF POPULATION
ONLINE IN EACH REGION

	2005	2010	2015
Africa	2%	10%	21%
Americas	36%	49%	66%
Arab States	8%	24%	37%
Asia and Pacific	9%	23%	37%
Commonwealth of Independent States	10%	34%	60%
Europe	46%	67%	78%

Source: International Telecommunications Union 2015.

Internet, but that the digital divide remains rather large. For example, three out of four Europeans, but less than 20 percent of Africans, have online access. Asia, with more than half of the world's population but with only one in three persons connected, is poised for dramatic increases in connectivity in the years ahead, as its economies continue to grow.

Individual motives for specific forms of cybercrime are as varied as the crimes themselves. Moreover, the motivation for a particular cyber-crime may be complex, or mixed. Hacking, and what might be called cybervandalism, is often the work of the curious, the adventurous, or the attention seeking. Many hackers are motivated by curiosity, to see just how far they can venture into cyberspace. Some hackers have spoken of a feeling of exhilaration when obtaining access to a previously secure system. Many of them, such as "Mafia Boy," seek to bask in their own notoriety by boasting of their exploits to peers.

In the case of financial crimes, in cyberspace as in terrestrial space, the motive is usually greed. Lust is reflected by the ubiquity of sexually explicit websites (entirely legal in some jurisdictions but forbidden in others). Rebellion often underlies efforts to inflict damage on symbols of power, whether the White House, McDonald's, or the Yasukuni Shrine in Tokyo (McNicol 2005). Revenge may be seen in theft or damage inflicted on an institution's information systems by a disgruntled employee or former employee.

The reader will already have noticed that the motives for computer crime outlined earlier are by no means modern phenomena, unique to the digital age. Greed, lust, power, curiosity, rebellion, revenge, and the desire for celebrity (or notoriety) are as old as recorded human history, and they are deeply engrained in the human behavioral repertoire. If there is anything new about motivations for cybercrime, it is the desire to master complex systems.

Motives may or may not be weakened or tempered by technological factors. Cybercriminals rarely have direct face-to-face contact with their victims, who, if they appear at all, do so as disembodied digits—0's and 1's. The air of unreality and the illusion of anonymity that characterize the environment of the typical cyber offender may have a disinhibiting effect.

OPPORTUNITIES

As was the case with the supply of motivated offenders, the availability of targets or prospective victims is also a function of the take-up of digital technology. Beyond the exponential increase in the number of individual users, the increasing connectivity of computers and communications and the pervasiveness of computers in Western industrial societies mean that more and more institutions and services depend on digital technology. It has been over two decades since someone observed that "everything depends on software" (Edwards 1995). Institutions of critical infrastructure such as electric power, water supply, telecommunications, air traffic control, and banking are all networked. An increasing volume of commerce occurs online. Most readers will deal with ATMs and online banking rather than with human tellers in bank branches. Books, software, music, and video are all available for purchase electronically. Online auctions such as eBay process millions of transactions daily. Social media such as Twitter and YouTube have hundreds of millions of users. Facebook has over a billion monthly users, and there are over a billion domain names on the Internet (Dewey 2014).

The basic idea is that each new technology, from the Internet, to the World Wide Web, to encryption, to wireless networks, to social media, can be exploited for criminal purposes. And each new application, from Internet chat rooms, to electronic funds transfer, to online share trading, to the use of one's credit card for Internet purchases, presents a new opportunity for someone to commit crime.

People who disclose their vacation plans on a publicly accessible social media site may, by advertising their absence, become more vulnerable to burglary. Others who reveal personal details (intimate or otherwise) may attract stalkers or others bent on harassment. To be sure, full citizenship in twenty-first-century democracies almost *demands* an online presence. But gratuitous exposure to risk is unwise in cyberspace, no less than on the ground. The problem is particularly difficult for children, whose naiveté and curiosity make them particularly vulnerable to predators. Given the rapid take-up of social media, it is perhaps not surprising that in the United Kingdom, related crime increased nearly eightfold between 2008 and 2012 (*The Guardian* 2012).

In the world of terrestrial crime, some targets are more vulnerable than others. The term "target hardening" is used to refer to measures employed to block criminal opportunities. So one sees deadlocks on doors and windows, engine immobilizers on motor vehicles, and bulletproof glass. The same principles apply in cyberspace, where a variety of technologies have been developed to reduce computer systems' vulnerability to criminal exploitation. These include firewalls, antivirus software, blocking and filtering technologies, encryption, and a variety of access controls from passwords to biometric authentication systems.

The basic challenge of opportunity reduction in cyberspace, as on the ground, is to minimize inconvenience to legitimate users while maximizing the effort required on the part of criminals. Like much in life, this requires a tradeoff. In the earliest days of the Internet, people left their doors unlocked, so to speak; most were not concerned if their "neighbors" came in and wandered around. Today, with significant assets to protect, and with many potential criminals lying in wait, you ignore system security at your peril.

GUARDIANS

The third element of routine activity theory and sine qua non of cybercrime is the absence of capable guardians. By this we mean someone (or something) to "mind the store." In the terrestrial world, capable guardianship may be exercised by *living people*, such as parents, teachers, the police officer (or private security guard) on the corner, or by *technological applications* such as burglar alarms, or CCTV cameras in stores, offices, or public places. The basic function of a guardian is to exercise surveillance over people and places for the purpose of preventing crime or to enable prompt response in the event that a crime is committed. So it is with capable guardianship in cyberspace. Parents monitor their children's use of the Internet, to insure that they do not venture into places that would make them vulnerable to victimization, or to offending. Employers monitor employees' use of their organization's information systems to guard against electronic misconduct ranging from sexual harassment, to exposing the system to viruses, to wasting time on the job. Systems administrators keep an eye open for unauthorized access or malicious code that can shut down or seriously degrade the capacity of a computer network. Technological means of capable guardianship in cyberspace are abundant. For example, standard Windows software systematically records websites that have been visited. Intrusion detection programs identify hacking attempts. Encryption technology enables one to conceal information from those for whom it is not intended.

Of course, would-be guardians do not always function the way they should. Parents may be lacking in computer literacy or may be careless in supervising their children. Computer users may be nonchalant about the sites that they visit and about the e-mail attachments that they open. They may use passwords that are easy to guess, or they may even leave them in plain view. They may fail to install or to update their virus detection software.

In the earliest days of the digital age, people were fairly relaxed about information security. The Internet was designed as an information commons; people were not terribly concerned about ownership or privacy. Software was designed for user friendliness and ease of interface rather than for security. The diffusion of digital technology and its application throughout individual and organizational life brought change. Opportunity reduction and stricter guardianship are becoming more common, and none too soon.

[5]

INCIDENCE, PREVALENCE, DISTRIBUTION, AND IMPACTS

If statistics of ordinary crime are but an imperfect reflection of the actual incidence of crime, statistics of cybercrime should be interpreted with even greater caution. Even the question "Is there more or less cybercrime than there was last year?" is difficult to answer. The reasons behind this sorry state of affairs are numerous and complex.

Just as terrestrial crime has its "dark figure" (offences that are not reported to police), so too does cybercrime. The reasons for nonreporting are similar in many respects. In some instances, the victim or victims may not even be aware that they have experienced a crime. Victims of successful charitable contribution frauds are left feeling good about themselves, not knowing that their "contribution" has gone to a criminal rather than to those truly in need. Other victims of cybercrime may also remain ignorant of their unfortunate circumstances. The unwitting user whose computer has been compromised and used in a botnet may never become aware of the crime. (Silva et al. [2013] report that the TDL4 botnet infected up to 4.5 million computers in 2011.) The stealthy nature of botnet infection was presumably imperceptible to many of the victims.

Some victims of crime do not report crimes because they regard the offence as too trivial, or because they believe the police will not be able to do anything about it. Patently fraudulent solicitations, if they are not screened out by a spam filter to begin with, are routinely relegated to the electronic "recycle bin," never to be reported. Few users of the Internet have been able to avoid receiving e-mail variations on the classic Nigerian advance fee fraud letter, asking for assistance in (and offering a commission for) moving a large amount of cash. Most recipients of such messages erase them and do not bother to report them to police.

Victims may be inclined to seek a quick remedy, rather than mobilize the law. When vandals snap my car radio antenna, I replace it, and get on with my life. Few recipients of "phishing" spams report them. When I receive a message from a "bank" asking me to confirm my account and PIN numbers, I erase it. Indeed, on all but a single occasion, the "financial institution" seeking my account details has been one with which I have never held an account! So it is that millions of attempts at fraud are committed daily, but only a few are called to the attention of the authorities. A recent survey of European Internet users found that more frequent users who have experienced a cybercrime are inclined to contact the website, an Internet service provider, or a vendor rather than the police. Overall, these findings suggest that the more knowledgeable a person is about cybercrime, the more likely he or she is to contact someone other than the police, at least with regard to relatively minor offences (European Commission 2015, p. 93).

On the other hand, victims of some cybercrimes may be disinclined to report because they fear retaliation from the offender. This is especially the case with cases of online harassment, where offenders have been known to redouble their efforts when their offensive communications have been called to the attention of the authorities (Citron 2014).

This reluctance to report to law enforcement agencies may extend to even the more serious financial cybercrimes. Financial institutions, desirous of preserving their reputations for security, may be reluctant to report losses to police, lest they receive embarrassing adverse publicity. Individual victims of cybercrime may be reluctant to report for fear of humiliation, or because they regard such a course of action as futile. For their part, police seek to foster alertness on the part of the public, as they do with terrestrial crime. This is particularly the case with so-called high-volume, low-value offences where the individual loss may be minor, but the aggregate of losses may be substantial indeed.

Problems surrounding the dark figure of cybercrime are compounded by the nature of digital technology, and by the administrative difficulties in producing comprehensible crime statistics. In the digital age, we must realize that software is not always perfect, and that "glitches" and "bugs"

INNOCENT EXPLANATIONS FOR COMPUTER MISADVENTURES

There is an Australian saying that if one is seeking an explanation for an adverse event, it is more likely to arise from a screw-up than from a conspiracy. This is often the case with computer mishaps. The original "bugs" in computing were real insects (although the term had been used previously to refer to industrial and electrical defects more generally; Shapiro 1987). Telephone service in one rural US community was once disrupted, not by a hacker, but by a farmer who unknowingly cut an underground telephone cable while trying to bury a dead cow. I was, on two separate occasions, single-handedly responsible for crashing the computer system at the Australian Institute of Criminology. In both instances, my modus operandi was to leave a space after a comma in an internal e-mail message sent to multiple addressees. This was entirely unintentional, the result of my lack of manual dexterity. The result was to overload the system with messages. The Institute soon upgraded its e-mail system to one that was more robust.

appear from time to time. Whether a malfunction occurs "naturally" or whether it is induced by foul play may not be immediately apparent. When cybercrime is reported to police, systems for recording the reports may be imperfect or nonexistent.

Even when a cybercrime does come to police attention, a number of factors may militate against its being formally recorded. Police may be preoccupied with a heavy caseload of serious terrestrial crimes. As such, they may be less likely to record what they perceive to be a relatively minor incident, for which evidence may not be readily available, and an offender difficult to identify. Police may also lack the resources and the capacity to deal with computer crime. Some officers of the "old school," who are more comfortable when they are looking angry men in the eye, regard computer forensics as something other than "real police work." (Goodman 1997). Where police lack the interest or the capacity effectively to investigate a reported cybercrime, they may simply relegate it to the "too hard basket."

This will change for the better with the passage of time, as current and future generations of police recruits will have grown up with digital technology. For the time being, there remains a digital divide within and between police agencies, just as there is within and between countries.

The United Nations Office on Drugs and Crime (UNODC 2013) published a comprehensive study of cybercrime in 2013, which included a survey of UN member states regarding their compilation of cybercrime statistics. Only sixty-nine states responded, and of those, fewer than 40 percent reported that recorded statistics of cybercrime were available for their jurisdiction.

The very nature of cybercriminal activity makes the production of crime statistics even more problematic. As we have seen, many cybercrimes are traditional crimes committed with twenty-first-century instruments. Fraud, embezzlement, stalking, bullying, destruction of property, gambling, possessing or disseminating offensive text or images—and a variety of other offences—are often charged and prosecuted under statutes that preceded the digital age. Statistics often reflect the substantive nature of the crime, rather than the technologies or instruments with which it was committed.

Efforts to quantify cybercrime are plagued by some of the same issues that confront "conventional" crime statistics, and then some. The conventional rule of "one victim, one offence" is strained in the digital age by technologies that enable one to rent a botnet consisting of a thousand compromised computers and then to transmit a fraudulent solicitation to a million recipients.

Beside statistics of crime reported to, and then recorded by, police, estimates of the incidence of cybercrime may be derived from sample surveys. These tend to ask individuals, or responsible persons within business organizations or government agencies, whether they or their organization had been the victim of any specific criminal activity.

Not all countries have both the resources and inclination to measure cybercrime. Some have one, but not the other. In the United States, the two main platforms for crime statistics are the Uniform Crime Reports (UCR) compiled and published by the FBI, and the National Crime Victims Survey (NCVS) managed by the Bureau of Justice Statistics. The UCR system is based on the substantive nature of the offences in question and does not refer to the instruments with which they are committed.

The NCVS is fielded annually and is based on a national sample of approximately 90,000 households. It too tends to focus on substantive crime types. Occasionally, it is accompanied by a supplementary questionnaire relating to some aspect of cybercrime. Such was the case in 2012 with an identity theft supplement (ITS). This supplement was also broad in scope, embracing a variety of means by which the identity data were acquired, such as physical theft and rummaging through waste bins. Online methods of theft were included among these means but were not subject to analysis in the published report (Harrell and Langton 2013).

A National Computer Security Survey (NCSS) was fielded by the RAND Corporation in 2006 on behalf of the US Department of Justice. Based on a sample of 36,000 businesses across thirty-six industry sectors in the United States, the survey sought to assess the experiences of respondent organizations during 2005. Unfortunately, a response rate of only 23 percent was achieved, significantly detracting from the generalizability of the findings; 58 percent of responding businesses reported experiencing a cyberattack of some kind, primarily involving a computer virus; 11 percent reported having been the victim of a cybertheft, generally embezzlement or fraud. Businesses responding to the survey reported $867 million in monetary losses (Rantala 2008).

The British Crime Survey (BCS), a nationally representative survey of private households in England and Wales, began sampling citizens to measure the incidence of criminal victimization in 1982. Since renamed the Crime Survey for England and Wales, it is arguably the most rigorous accounting of crime victimization conducted by any government. In 2002, for the first time, the BCS included questions related to computer crime (Allen et al. 2005). In that year, 18.2 percent of respondents with an Internet connection at home reported that their computer had been affected by a computer virus in the previous 12 months. Only about a third reported it to anyone, and the police were notified in less than 1 percent of cases. Twelve percent reported having received an e-mail that they regarded as offensive or threatening. And 2.2 percent of respondents reported that someone else had gained access to their computers; none were reported to police. Unfortunately, collection of statistics on cybercrime was suspended pending further research and development of measurement methods (Office of National Statistics 2014).

Among the more impressive attempts to measure the incidence of cybercrime are the large-scale population "Eurobarometer" surveys fielded by the European Commission. Annual surveys conducted since 2012 (European Commission 2012, 2014, 2015) have each asked more than 25,000 respondents about their concerns and experiences with different types of cybercrime. The surveys have been drafted with a view toward comparability over time and across member states. The Eurobarometer surveys are also useful in measuring levels of concern (and changes over time in that concern) about specific cybercrime issues such as security of online payments; misuse of personal data; not receiving goods ordered online; and precautionary measures taken by respondents, such as password use and installation of antivirus software. Levels of concern for most crime types increased from 2013 to 2014.

The two most common cybercrime experiences reported by European internet users were finding malicious software on their device (47 percent) and receiving communications requesting (with apparent fraudulent intent) login access to their computer, or personal details (31 percent). In addition, 14 percent of users reported they had been denied access to online services because of cyberattacks, 12 percent had their social media or e-mail account hacked, and 12 percent have experienced online sales fraud. Across the European Union, 8 percent of Internet users reported having been asked for payment in return for regaining control of their device, 8 percent claimed to have been a victim of credit card or banking fraud online, 7 percent reported being the victim of identity theft, and 7 percent reported having accidentally encountered child pornography online. Consistent with routine activity theory, daily Internet users in Europe are more likely than less frequent users to have experienced or been a victim of most of the various types of cybercrime (European Commission 2015, p. 77).

A variety of organizations and agencies publish statistics of those cybercrimes affecting their own commercial or policy interests. However, not all organizations and agencies that publish crime statistics or survey results are disinterested. Some may have a vested interest in overestimating the incidence and cost of cybercrime, while others may be inclined to minimize the problem. This is not to suggest that all commercial and nongovernmental interests are necessarily biased in their disclosures, but the risk of departure from objectivity is undeniable.

There exist other specialized avenues for reporting cybercrime. Special "hotlines" exist in some jurisdictions for the reporting of child pornography. In New Zealand, for example, the Child Alert Hotline is sponsored by ECPAT New Zealand (an NGO dedicated to child protection issues) and the Censorship Compliance Unit of the NZ Department of Internal Affairs. Some financial institutions invite their customers to forward suspicious e-mail using the company's name directly to the company.[1] Subscribers to services of computer emergency response teams (CERTs) are able to report incidents and seek remedial assistance as part of their subscription services (AusCERT 2015). An Australian Cybercrime Online Reporting Network (ACORN) was introduced in 2015 to facilitate reporting of cybercrime from across the Australian federal system, as well as to provide advice relating to prevention and to response in the aftermath of a criminal incident.

The Internet Crime Complaint Center (I3C) is a partnership between the US Federal Bureau of Investigation (FBI) and the National White Collar Crime Center (NW3C). Formerly known as the Internet Fraud Complaint Center, I3C publishes scam alerts and other advice relating to cybersecurity. I3C annual reports present statistics on the total number of complaints received per year, the total losses experienced by those victims who lodged a report, and the US state jurisdictions and foreign countries from which the complaints originated. Comparability of data is questionable; at best, one obtains a fragmented picture of frauds. Some specialized organizations report statistics relevant to their goals and objectives. The Anti-Phishing Working Group (2014) reported 123,741 unique phishing attacks worldwide during the second quarter of 2014.

The meaning of hotline data depends not only on the incidence of the criminal conduct in question but also on the victim's awareness of the crime, the accessibility of the available medium of reporting, and the victim's inclination to report.

As noted earlier, a great deal of computer-related crime really involves digital technology as instrumental to, or incidental to, a conventional offence such as fraud, extortion, or drug dealing. When these offences are counted in police statistics, they are usually classified in accordance with the nature of the substantive offence, not the means by which the offence was committed. So extortion is extortion, whether the threat was communicated in longhand or via e-mail. Whether plans for a drug deal are made over the Internet, or records of the deal are stored in digital form, is irrelevant to the principal charge. Suffice it to say that a large proportion of computer-related crimes are never enumerated as such.

IMPACTS OF CYBERCRIME

The actual or potential impact of computer crime can be serious indeed. To the extent that people have become dependent upon, if not addicted to, digital technology, any disruption or degradation of information systems can be extremely costly, as well as annoying. In addition to the extrinsic costs of computer crime, there may be certain intrinsic costs borne by victims as well. While relatively few readers may have felt the fear instilled by a stalker, many if not most will have lost a few hours of work as the result of malicious code. The panic of losing data, whether as a result of foul play, system malfunction, or negligence, is a nontrivial experience. Extend this across a large organization or network, and the losses, extrinsic and intrinsic, add up.

In addition to the loss of those assets that may have been stolen, companies may sustain a disruption of business operations, damage to corporate reputation, the cost of remediating damage to systems, and the expenses entailed in enhancing their information security regime. Depending upon the nature of their business, other outlays may weigh heavily. Replacing the compromised credit cards of millions of customers can be extremely costly.

Although quantification of computer crime and its financial impact is often fraught with hyperbole and wild speculation, some degree of rigor is being brought to the task.

Calculating costs incurred as the result of such attacks is always risky; the estimated losses to businesses worldwide from the "I Love You" virus ranged from $6.7 billion to $15.3 billion in computer downtime and software damage (Grossman 2000; Beh 2001).

There are more insidious costs to be reckoned with. Another consequence of the digital age, of relevance to law-abiding citizens and cyber-criminals alike, is the enormous capacity for surveillance that digital technology places in the hands of governments and private organizations. Ordinary computer users leave their tracks all over cyberspace. It is possible, using data mining technologies, to build extensive electronic

COSTS OF CYBERCRIME

Some estimates of the extent or cost of e-commerce crime are provided by Crimmins et al. (2014) and by Newman and Clarke (2003).

Security measures put in place in the aftermath of the JP Morgan Chase hack of 2014 were reported to cost $250 million *per year* (CNBC 2014).

Following the Target hack of 2014, the cost of replacing compromised credit cards alone was estimated at $200 million (Chaudhuri 2014).

The "I Love You" virus was estimated to have cost users worldwide from $6.7 billion to $15.3 billion for lost data, lost business, lost productivity, and costs of remediation.

The person who released the Melissa virus acknowledged in his plea agreement that the virus caused $80 million in damage. Other estimates of loss approached $400 million.

The cost of the Mafia Boy DDOS attacks was estimated as approaching $1.2 billion.[2]

dossiers. Official reactions to cybercrime often entail a greater willingness and ability to compile databases of personal information and to intercept private communications. It has been reported that the Chinese government employs 100,000 individuals who regularly monitor e-mail traffic. Disclosures by Edward Snowden in 2013 revealed that the US National Security Agency had established a massive data collection program called PRISM, which captures vast amounts of data, including e-mail voice, social media, and file transfers (Greenwald 2014). It was reported in 2014 that the NSA developed the capacity to share more than 850 billion records with more than 1,000 analysts at twenty-three US Government agencies by means of a search engine called "IC REACH." The system was designed to provide access to the communications of non-US persons, but it appears to allow incidental recovery of US citizens' data as well (Gallagher 2014). The impacts of this pervasive surveillance on the spontaneity and freedom of expression that are so essential to citizens of a democracy remain to be seen.

In contrast to the underestimation of the *incidence* of crime involving digital technology, estimates of the *costs* of computer crime are vulnerable to inflation. In most modern jurisdictions, where law enforcement and prosecutorial resources are finite, the relative seriousness of a crime may determine whether it receives official attention. A victim who values police attention may well place the most generous possible construction on the losses he or she may have sustained at the hands of a cybercriminal.

Unless they choose to conceal their victimization, some industries go to great lengths to estimate their losses. This is especially so when they prefer that government authorities place the interests of the industry high on the public agenda. The rigor of some estimates may at times be called into question.

The Business Software Alliance claimed the commercial value of unlicensed PC software installations totaled $62.7 billion globally in 2013 (BSA 2013). It estimated that 43 percent of all software installed in 2013 was unlicensed. It may come as no surprise that those nations with the highest rates of piracy (Zimbabwe, Moldova, Georgia, all with rates at or over 90 percent) are from the developing world, while those with the lowest piracy rates (Japan, United States, Luxembourg, with rates of 20 percent or less) are among the most affluent.

A 2003 survey of 333 online merchants in North America revealed that revenue loss arising from online credit card fraud was 1.3 percent. Based on the level of business to consumer online sales, this was estimated at $1.6 billion for the year. A 2014 estimate reported a stable loss rate of 0.9 percent since 2010.[3]

A survey of public and private sector organizations in Australia, modeled to some extent on the US Computer Crime and Security Survey, revealed that one-third of respondents had experienced a cyberattack in the past year, a slight decline from previous surveys (AusCERT 2005). Infections from worms, viruses, and Trojans were the most common form of attack. The report further observed that attacks motivated by financial gain were increasing both in volume and in sophistication.

Given the proliferation of vested interests in state, commercial, and nonprofit sectors, it is perhaps not surprising that a good deal of discourse on the cost of cybercrime contains more than a small dose of hyperbole. At the end of the day, one should approach statistics of cybercrime with extreme caution. At the very least, one should seek to determine the assumptions that underlie various estimates. To the extent that it is possible, objective, dispassionate discussion should be encouraged, and welcomed. Among the most rigorous efforts of this kind to date has been the work of Anderson et al. (2012).

In any discussion of the costs of cybercrime, it is useful to distinguish between the direct financial losses sustained by victims of an offense and the indirect costs resulting from efforts employed to prevent cyber offences from occurring (or reoccurring). One might also consider intangible or unquantifiable losses, such as psychological harm experienced by victims, or reputational damage suffered by organizations.

Anderson et al. make the intriguing observation that the costs of IT security appear substantially to exceed the direct cost of cybercrime, while a relatively small percentage of offenders is responsible for a disproportionately large volume of offences. Accordingly, they argue that it would make good economic sense to invest more in "up-front" law enforcement.

CYBERCRIME OFFENDERS AND VICTIMS

What kinds of people commit cybercrime? What kinds of people fall victim to cybercrimes? Cybercriminals, and their victims, are very diverse groups. The stereotypic image of the geek, barricaded in his bedroom surrounded by empty soft drink cans and soggy pizza cartons, belies the varied reality of offending. And the likelihood of becoming the victim of a cybercrime is often the product of lifestyle choices or exposure to risk. Given the diversity of cybercrime, it should come as no surprise that there is no such thing as a "typical" cybercrime offender or victim. Offender and victim characteristics will vary according to crime type.

Offenders

Some of the most accomplished hackers, whether they work on their own, in criminal groups, or for governments, are nothing short of brilliant. One might include participants in *Dark Market* and the *Olympic Games* attack on Iranian nuclear enrichment facilities in this category (Glenny 2011; Zetter 2014). But these high-end practitioners are exceptional. Lower on the scale are the so-called Script Kiddies, who download hacker tools from the Web and follow the instructions that come with them. At the very bottom of the scale are those individuals, apparently from digitally disadvantaged countries, whose fraudulent overtures reflect a very low level of literacy. In between these polar extremes are more ordinary souls. The "democratization" of cybercrime has been facilitated by the ready accessibility of hacker tools and other facilitative technologies, which are quite user-friendly and well within the financial means of ordinary users. In general, statistics on cybercrime do not represent a perfect mirror of criminal propensity; rather, they reflect the reality that all else equal, the less skilled the offender, the greater the likelihood of getting caught.

Because of the resources devoted to the investigation of online sex offenses, it is not surprising that considerable attention has been devoted to the characteristics of online sex offenders. Motivans and Kyckelhahn (2007) reported statistics on 1,275 individuals charged with offences relating to child pornography in 2006, 97 percent of which involved use of a computer. Eighty-nine percent of the offenders were Caucasian, 99 percent were male, and 58 percent had attended some college. Their median age was forty-two, with most aged between twenty-five and fifty. Most were employed, and 80 percent had no previous felony convictions. A smaller survey of 101 US federal child pornography offenders (Burgess, Carretta, Carrie, and Burgess 2012) noted that 19.6 percent of the offenders had themselves experienced sexual abuse, and 10.8 percent physical abuse. Over one-third (36.3 percent) revealed a history of psychiatric treatment. Babchishin et al. (2011) published a meta-analysis of online sex offenders, including child pornography offenders and those seeking illicit contact with children. The twenty-seven separate studies comprised a total of 4,844 individual cases, primarily from the United States, United Kingdom, and Canada. Online offenders were more likely to be Caucasian, slightly younger, unemployed, never married, and to have experienced more physical and sexual abuse than both the general population and "terrestrial" sex offenders.

Crime statistics in China are not widely published, but online fraud appears to be the most common cybercrime type in that country. Chan and Wang (2015) reported findings from court records in Souzhou and Guangdong that suggest over 90 percent of offenders were male. Most were between the ages of 18 and 35 years, and nearly half had some college education. Forty percent of the Souzhou offenders were unemployed.

Victims

Cybercrime victims, too, are a diverse group. Large organizations are at risk because of the values that they symbolize and for the digital assets they control. State agencies may be targets of protest or attractive for the intelligence data that they possess.

It borders on tautology to suggest that individual victims of cybercrime tend to have placed themselves in a position of greater exposure to risk. Users with a high online profile may attract harassment; those who engage in extensive online banking and commercial activity are more vulnerable to phishing and identity theft.

In the terrestrial world, a disproportionate number of victims themselves have a criminal record. Cyberspace, as it turns out, is no different. Holt and Bossler (2014), and Holt et al. (2015, p. 304) summarize a number of studies and conclude that those who engage in hacking, piracy, and bullying, among other offences, are also at greater risk of victimization.

Almost by definition, victims of fraud might be characterized as greedy and gullible; victims of romance fraud lonely rather than greedy. When discussing cybercrime victimization, it may be useful to think in terms of those who are targeted directly, as opposed to those whose victimization has been mediated or routed through an institution. An individual who receives a personalized harassing or threatening message is victimized directly. On the other hand, one whose credit card details are stolen from the servers of a financial institution or e-retailer experiences indirect victimization. Of course, to be victimized indirectly is hardly any consolation. It makes little difference if images of one in revealing poses are disseminated after having been snatched from one's own computer, or from some collective, but ill-guarded storage facility in "the cloud."

The difference between direct and indirect victimization lies in the locus of responsibility for one's misfortune. Failure to secure one's own system with basic security software is personally less excusable than being let down by a major financial institution to whom you have entrusted your digital assets (assuming you have taken reasonable precautions to safeguard PIN and password details).

Conversely, an organization, private or public, can be let down by its employees. A worker's harassment of a fellow employee many expose the employer to liability for failing to ensure a safe workplace. Through a technique known as "spear phishing," employees of an organization may be the recipients of a message that appears to be from a fellow employee or other trusted source. Upon opening the message, the unwitting employee may allow in a virus that can infect the entire system.

Holt et al. (2015, p. 304) provide a useful overview of the literature on the risk of cybercrime victimization. Their summary concludes that individuals who are frequent users of social media and who spend more time online in places like chat rooms are more likely to be targeted for bullying or harassment. They also note that users who themselves have committed cybercrime, or whose friends have done so, are more likely to be victimized. These general patterns are similar to terrestrial risk factors and are consistent with routine activity theory (see also Holt and Bossler, 2009). Holt et al. (2014) surveyed a representative sample of Singapore youth to test routine activity theory as a predictor of victimization by cyber and mobile phone bullying. They found that home Internet access, and time spent in chat room, bulletin board, and blog use, increased the risk of victimization. This was particularly the case for those who had experienced physical bullying. Females were also more likely to be victimized.

Based on a Eurobarometer survey of 26,593 respondents in twenty-seven European countries, Williams (2015) found that the greater one's access to public Internet facilities, and the greater one's involvement in selling on online auction sites, the greater the risk of identity theft. He also reported a curvilinear relationship between affluence and risk: those at least risk of victimization were persons of average socioeconomic status.

Buchanan and Whitty (2014) studied online romance frauds using two samples. The first was a sample of subscribers (primarily UK residents) to an online dating site; the second was from a support site for victims (primarily US residents) of romance fraud. Victims were primarily middle aged and harbored more intense romantic beliefs than nonvictims. The authors concluded that demographic variables and sexual orientation were poor predictors of victimization.

With data from the 2006 US National Crime Victimization Survey, Nobles et al. (2014) compared victims of cyberstalking with "terrestrial" stalking victims. They found the cyber victims to be slightly younger; a greater percentage was white and male, and reported significantly higher levels of income and education.

The prominence accorded cybercrime committed against high-visibility targets in the world's wealthier nations makes it easier to ignore the fact that, in general, the risk of cybercrime victimization is greater in the world's developing nations. The United States hosts some of the world's largest and most powerful commercial institutions and government agencies. In addition, its authoritative and influential media organizations give prominent coverage to cybercrime.

On the underprivileged side of the digital divide, individuals and organizations may not be able to afford the most effective up-to-date security technologies. Moreover, state capacity to respond to reported cybercrime may be weak or nonexistent. It follows therefore that this relative deficit in guardianship will be reflected in higher rates of victimization. According to the UN Office on Drugs and Crime, with the exception of credit card fraud, cybercrime victimization rates are generally higher in countries with lower levels of economic development (UNODC 2103, p. 6).

Table 4.1 in Chapter 4 provides a snapshot of this distribution. What is new in a highly "wired" country may not yet appear on the radar screen of a country that has just entered the digital age. This, of course, does have its blessings for some. Countries that are lagging in the uptake of digital technology can learn from the experiences of the digitally advantaged. But there is a downside. Countries that are "digitally challenged" may still lack the capacity to defend themselves against cybercriminal exploitation. What limited assets they have will be even more vulnerable. Although details are understandably sketchy, it was alleged some years ago that cybercriminals nearly succeeded in transferring the assets of the national bank of a small island nation into their own accounts elsewhere.

And just as transnational organized criminals are able to use weak and failing states as "criminal havens" so too may digitally challenged countries serve as "*cyber*criminal havens."

TRENDS IN CYBERCRIME

A number of basic trends in cybercrime have emerged or have intensified in recent years. The first is *sophistication*. Cybercrime is becoming more sophisticated, in terms of planning and organization. Over a decade ago, Thompson (2004) described the highly creative virus writers who design malicious code of great complexity. Here are some general examples:

- The speed with which viruses infect computers around the world has increased dramatically since the turn of the century. In 2001, the Code Red Virus infected 150,000 computer systems in fourteen hours. A mere two months later, the NIMDA virus spread across the United States in just one hour, attacking 86,000 computers (The White House 2003). In 2003, the Slammer worm compromised 75,000 computers in ten minutes.
- Malicious code may be designed to "mutate" over time, changing itself with each successive run but maintaining its original function. This is designed to conceal the code from detection by antivirus programs. Such code is sometimes referred to as "polymorphic malware."
- Hacking tools are becoming more powerful and easier to use. The term "intelligent malware" has been used to describe malicious code that seeks out vulnerable systems and/or covers its own tracks.
- Distributed denial of service (DDOS) attacks have become considerably more powerful. In 2014, an attack reaching nearly 400 gigabits per second was directed against servers in France. It was engineered using 4,529 servers running on 1,298 different networks (Vaughan-Nichols 2014).

- Web pages may be counterfeit in a manner such that the fake will be indistinguishable from the original legitimate page. The fake page may communicate false or misleading information in furtherance of an investment solicitation, or it may contain infectious software to compromise an unwitting visitor's computer.
- Techniques of "Phishing" have been refined where apparently legitimate Web links are placed in an e-mail message. When activated, the site will mimic a genuine Web page and invite the visitor to confirm his or her account and PIN numbers. Phishing overtures may now be more subtle and more precisely targeted at members of a particular organization, and made to appear as if they came from a trusted coworker.

The identification and acquisition of valid credit card details have become automated. In years past, a hacker would download customers' credit card details from the system of a large retailer, only to find that many of the accounts in question had been cancelled or had expired. More recently, sniffer programs have been inserted into a large retailer's servers to seek out and store data from recent transactions. The programs then automatically encrypt, compress, and forward the valid data to a computer designated by the hacker (Verini 2010).

The Stuxnet virus, as noted earlier, was arguably the most complex and sophisticated malware developed to date (Zetter 2014). As it turns out, Stuxnet was not unique, and variations of the Stuxnet model have been active for some time. In 2015, the information security firm Kaspersky Labs reported that malware deeply embedded in computer systems in Russia, Pakistan, China, Afghanistan, Iran, and elsewhere contains surveillance, decryption, and sabotage tools that defy existing security controls and antivirus products. The malware has been inserted in the "firmware," the basic read-only memory installed in a computing device at the time of manufacture. Kaspersky sources implied that the activity in question, which had occurred since 2001, has been undertaken by the US National Security Agency and US Cyber Command (Sanger and Perlroth 2015b).

Another illustration of the unprecedented sophistication of recent cybercrimes can be seen in a bank theft that came to public attention in February 2015. Over a two-year period, a group of hackers had obtained access to the computer systems of more than one hundred banks and financial institutions in over thirty countries around the world. By sending infected e-mails that were opened by employees, the hackers inserted malicious software into the systems of the target institutions and then studied the daily routines of the banks. This enabled them to operate unobtrusively within the banks' systems. The theft took two basic forms. In one, funds were transferred to accounts that the hackers had opened in other banks around the world. In the other, ATMs were directed to dispense cash at certain times and places where accomplices were positioned to remove the money. The total amount stolen was not immediately apparent, but it was reported to be at least $300 million (Sanger and Perlroth 2015a).

As noted earlier, increasingly sophisticated fraudulent overtures are targeted at particular market segments, such as academics. While it is flattering to be invited to deliver a keynote address to a conference in an exotic location, the more cautious scholar would be well advised not to rush to pay registration fees, notwithstanding any reassurance of future reimbursement. It is also common to claim the imprimatur of a legitimate, prestigious organization to add credibility to a fraudulent conference invitation. A number of these organizations have posted warnings to this end. The Brussels-based Union of International Associations posts apparently fraudulent conference-related solicitations on its Fraud Monitor website.[1]

Increased sophistication is also evident in the marketing of "Scareware" or "Ransomware." An ominous message that one's computer has been compromised, combined with an offer of a technological fix at a very reasonable price, preys upon the naïve user's anxiety and gullibility. The fix may be of no benefit, or, worse, it may facilitate the introduction of malicious software. Thus, the most trusting victims will purchase the software and thereby pay for the privilege of being serially defrauded (Giles 2010).

TECHNOLOGIES OF CONCEALMENT
Cryptography

The sophistication of cybercrime is compounded by the widespread availability of cryptography. Once the monopoly of military organizations and intelligence services, technologies for concealing the content of electronic communications from all but the intended recipient are now widely

CRIMINAL EXPLOITATION OF WIRELESS TECHNOLOGY

The advent of wireless technology, for all its benefits, is creating new criminal opportunities. Wireless local area networks (LANS) are vulnerable to penetration. The term "war driving" was coined to refer to the act of locating and logging wireless access points (or "hot spots") while in motion. Toward the end of 2003, one began to see prosecutions for unauthorized access to wireless systems from "mobile hackers." In November of that year, two men in Michigan were charged with cracking a home improvement store's nationwide network from a car parked outside one of the stores (US Department of Justice 2004c).

available. Encryption is ideally suited to those offenders who wish to communicate in furtherance of criminal conspiracies or who wish to conceal information that might be used against them in court. These might include records of criminal transactions or illicit images. In addition to cryptography and steganography, technologies enable individuals to conceal their identities online or to impersonate other users. These technologies make it very difficult to identify suspects (Morris 2004a).

TECHNOLOGIES OF ANONYMITY

A popular technology that facilitates concealment of online activity is TOR (an abbreviation of The Onion Router). This is an open network that facilitates anonymity and inhibits traffic analysis. Based on a distributed network of over 5,000 relays around the world, TOR makes it very difficult to trace one's online activity. Information is encrypted numerous times and then sent through a number of randomly selected relays at which the data are serially decrypted and sent to their final destination. TOR was used by whistleblower Edward Snowden to communicate with *The Guardian* newspaper.[2] TOR may not be entirely "bulletproof," as a number of websites hosting marketplaces for illicit products running on TOR were shut down in November 2014 (Wakefield, 2014).

COMMERCIALIZATION

The second major trend is *commercialization*. If crime does follow opportunity, you can be sure that where there is money to be made, cybercriminals will try their hand. Today, more and more commercial activity occurs
in an online environment. By definition, this creates an increasing number
of opportunities for criminal exploitation. It follows that the incidence of
cybercrime with a financial motive may be expected to increase.

Cyberspace illegalities that have not previously been characterized
by commercialism are becoming increasingly subject to financial motivation. Consider child pornography. The earliest forms of Internet
child pornography entailed noncommercial exchange or barter between collectors. Little if any commercial activity was evident (Grant,
David, and Grabosky 1997). More recently, commercial exchange has
become apparent, including service providers who are able and willing
to refer users to illicit content sites for a fee (BBC News 2002). Over
a decade ago, entrepreneurial children equipped with webcams operated commercial sites using credit card payment processing companies
to manage the revenue generated by their home-produced images and
online sexual performances (Eichenwald 2005). This has evolved into
what is now called Webcam Child Sex Tourism, which can be highly
profitable for adult entrepreneurs, but most unfortunate for children in
poor countries.

Similar patterns once characterized unauthorized access to computer
systems and the dissemination of malicious code. At the dawn of the digital age, hackers and virus writers were amateurs (albeit sometimes very
competent ones). Today the term "hackers for hire" is becoming more familiar, and there are those virus writers who work on a fee-for-service
basis (Goldstein 2015).

The ability to communicate instantly with millions of people at little or
no cost is not lost on legitimate marketers or on criminal fraudsters. If a
message sent to a million recipients elicits responses from a mere one-
tenth of 1 percent of them, this still adds up to one thousand prospective
victims. The collection and sale of active e-mail addresses serves a niche
market. There are entrepreneurs who harvest valid e-mail addresses for
sale to legitimate commercial interests as well as to criminals. "Botnets"
are rented out to spammers and phishers.

Hacker tools are freely available for downloading, but the better ones, some of which are designed expressly for malicious purposes, are now available for sale or rent. Not only can Zeus and Blackhole exploit kits be rented; lessors offer user support and may also provide regular updates as part of the service agreement (Oliver et al. 2012; Holt 2012). Botnets, and a range of other products and services to facilitate cybercrime, are also available for purchase or hire (Davidow 2013). These include encrypting malware to make them more difficult to detect; access to dedicated servers from which to launch attacks; programming services; virtual private network (VPN) services to ensure anonymity in communications; the modification of a program to disguise its purpose (obfuscation); and DDOS attack services (Alazab, Venkatraman, Watters, Alazab, and Alazab 2012; Goncharov 2012).

The growth of commercialization has been accompanied by the emergence of platforms to facilitate online commercial exchange. Glenny (2011) describes one of the more prominent "carders' markets" where stolen credit card details could be purchased in bulk. Hutchings and Holt (2014) compare thirteen such forums, where one may obtain stolen financial details, software and hardware to facilitate data theft, and related services such as money laundering. Many of the sites are located in Russia, a jurisdiction beyond the reach of foreign law enforcement agencies.

Another example of commercialization may be seen in the practice of searching for, and then selling, undiscovered flaws in computer code, known colloquially as "zero-day exploits." Not long ago it was common for altruistic hackers who came across such flaws to alert the manufacturer to the defects, in return for a note of thanks or perhaps a complimentary T-shirt. In recent years, the value of such information, which in some cases can facilitate clandestine access to computer systems, has become readily apparent not only to the manufacturers of the software in question but also to governments and to civilian predatory hackers. The entrepreneurial spirit is further apparent in the emergence of brokers who market the information for a percentage of the amount paid. A veritable bidding war has resulted, with some governments prepared to pay over $100,000 for exclusive information about a particular vulnerability; information regarding one flaw in an operating system reportedly sold for $500,000 (Perlroth and Sanger 2013). It was reported that in 2011, the US National Security Agency spent $25 million on "covert purchases of software vulnerabilities" (Sanger 2013). While those responsible for the aforementioned Olympic Games operation are disinclined to reveal details, it has been suggested that the attack on Iranian nuclear facilities was accomplished with the use of four separate zero-day exploits (Zetter 2014).

The numerous opportunities for criminal exploitation of cyberspace are not lost on traditional criminal organizations. One may expect to see organized crime embrace digital technology with increasing enthusiasm in the years ahead.

INTEGRATION

The third important trend in cybercrime is *integration*. As is the case with terrestrial crime, cybercrimes are not always committed in isolation. For example, armed robbers may steal a motor vehicle to travel to the scene of the robbery and to facilitate a getaway. So it is that certain types of cybercrime will entail a combination of different criminal acts. A recent development has seen the integration of distinct forms of computer crime to achieve synergies. Consider the following: Unsolicited electronic mail or "Spam" may contain malicious code that can be activated if the mail is opened or if the recipient clicks on a link (such as one that reads "Click Here for Free Teen Sex Pix"). This code can be designed so that, if activated, it will allow the offender to "commandeer" the infected computer and use it in furtherance of criminal purposes. This can entail recording the victim's password and credit card details, or it may entail directing the victim computer against another target. This latter scenario combines the scope of a virus infection with the intensity of a distributed denial of service attack. Such an attack may in turn be an element of extortion.

A number of additional trends in cybercrime are worth noting. These include the involvement of juveniles, the increasing diversity of cybercriminal organizations, the systematic violation of individual privacy by commercial and state actors alike, and the cross-border nature of much cybercrime.

THE INVOLVEMENT OF JUVENILES

The tremendous power that digital technology places in the hands of ordinary individuals extends to juveniles as well. Some of the more notorious cybercrimes have been committed by individuals of relatively tender years (DeMarco 2001). The criminal exploits of the Massachusetts teenager who disabled communications to the air traffic control tower at the Worcester Regional Airport, and the distributed denial of service attacks by Mafia Boy, were described earlier. The first juvenile ever incarcerated for cybercrime in the United States was Jonathan James, a fifteen year old from Florida who in 1999 gained unauthorized access to computers of the Defense Threat Reduction Agency. The following year he pleaded guilty and was sentenced to six months home detention.

In March 2004, another Massachusetts teenager went on an electronic rampage. He sent an e-mail to a Florida school that read:

> your all going to perish and flourish . . . you will all die
> Tuesday, 12:00 p.m.
> we're going to have a "blast"
> hahahahahaha wonder where I'll be? youll all be destroyed. im sick of your [expletive deleted]
> school and piece of [expletive deleted] staff, your all gonna [expletive deleted] die you pieces of crap!!!!
> DIE MOTHER [expletive deleted] IM GONA BLOW ALL YOU UP AND MYSELF
> ALL YOU NAZI LOVING MEXICAN FAGGOT BITCHES ARE DEAD" (US Department of Justice 2005d)

As a result of this threat, the school was closed for two days.

Five months later, the same juvenile obtained unauthorized access to the internal network of a major Internet service provider. In January 2005 he penetrated the internal system of a large telephone service provider, obtained information about one of the provider's customers, and posted it on the Internet. He also set up a number of telephone accounts without having to pay for them. Shortly thereafter, he used a portable wireless device to access the Internet and arranged with accomplices to communicate a bomb threat to a school in Massachusetts, necessitating the school's evacuation.

In June 2005, he contacted another telephone service provider which had terminated an account that a friend had fraudulently activated. He threatened to initiate a denial of service attack against the provider unless he was granted access to the provider's system. The demand was not met, and within ten minutes an attack was launched that succeeded in shutting down a good deal of the provider's web operations. After pleading guilty in a US Federal Court, the youth was sentenced to eleven months detention in a juvenile facility, followed by two years of supervised release. During these periods of detention and supervised release, he was prohibited from possessing or using any computer, cell phone, or other equipment with which to access the Internet (US Department of Justice 2005d).

The involvement of juveniles in deeds that, if they were even possible at all at the end of the twentieth century were almost exclusively the work of adults, is an intriguing development. Pontell and Rosoff (2009) have used the term "white-collar delinquency" to refer to this departure from the historical norm. It further complicates the problems of white-collar crime theorists, who note that persons of less than relatively high social status are committing a considerable amount of "white-collar" crime. White-collar delinquency also complicates the lives of prosecutors. US Federal prosecutors, who traditionally have had little occasion to charge juveniles, now find themselves having to seek terms of incarceration for young offenders in order to make it very clear that certain kinds of online activity are totally unacceptable.

ORGANIZED CYBERCRIME

While there are many hackers who work alone, for fun and/or profit, organized cybercrime has become more prominent in recent years. Goodman (2015) estimates that as much as 80 percent of nonstate cybercrime committed today is the work of organizations. But organized cybercrime belies the conventional image of organized crime, a hierarchical, ethnic-based group specializing in extortion and the provision of illicit goods and services. In the twenty-first century, cybercriminal organizations have become more complex and diverse. Today, organized cybercrime has long since given way to networks and to loose, temporary coalitions of individuals driven by diverse motives (Broadhurst, Grabosky, Alazab, and Chon 2014).

One does, however, still see large formal organizations involved in cybercrime. Much of this entails the work of governments (or their proxies), whom we have seen to be active in cyberespionage, and occasionally, in operations involving denial of service. While these activities may be permissible under one's own laws, they almost always violate the laws of the countries whose information has been compromised. The organizational forms of cybercrime tend to reflect crime type; certain structures are better suited to the commission of specific crimes. The idiom "horses for courses" applies here.

SWARMS

Swarms may be described as disorganized collectivities with temporary common purpose and without institutionalized leadership. Swarms tend to have minimal chains of command and may operate in viral forms in ways reminiscent of earlier "hacktivist" groups. Swarms seem to be most active in ideologically driven online activities such as hate crimes and political resistance. The group *Anonymous* illustrates a typical swarm-type group (Olson 2012).

HIERARCHIES

Some traditional organized crime groups, having recognized the applications of digital technology to criminal activity, appear to engage specialized expertise for the purpose. In the United States, members of the Gambino crime family were alleged to have produced false bar code labels and credit cards. An associate of the Bonnano family was charged with various offences involving digital technology, including fraud in connection with access devices (Choo and Grabosky 2013).

The more sophisticated cybercrime organizations are characterized by substantial functional specialization and division of labor. Chabinsky (2010) outlines the various roles that a major fraud conspiracy may entail:

1. *Executives* of the organization to select targets, recruit and assign members to various tasks, and manage the distribution of criminal proceeds
2. *Coders* or programmers to write the malware necessary to commit the crime
3. *Distributors* to trade and sell stolen data
4. *Technicians* to maintain the organization's infrastructure such as servers, Internet service providers, and encryption
5. *Hackers* to seek and exploit vulnerabilities in target systems and networks, in order to gain administrator access
6. *Fraud specialists* to develop and employ social engineering schemes

7. *Hosts* to provide "safe" facilities of illicit content servers, often through elaborate botnet and proxy networks
8. *Cashiers* to control drop accounts and manage individual cash couriers, or "money mules"
9. *Money mules* and tellers to transfer the proceeds of frauds to a secure location

NETWORKS

Those cybercrime groups whose activities entail the routine exchange of data tend to adopt a networked organizational form. The most prominent examples are those groups involved in the exchange of child pornography and those which engage in large-scale piracy of digital content.

Dreamboard was a very sophisticated, members-only group that exchanged illicit images of children. It vetted prospective members, required continuing contributions of illicit material as a condition of membership, and rewarded those who produced and shared their own content. Members achieved status levels reflecting the quantity and "quality" of their contributions. The group used aliases rather than their actual names; links to illicit content were encrypted and password protected. Access to the group's bulletin board was through proxy servers. These routed traffic through other computers in order to mask a member's true location, thereby impeding investigators from tracing the member's online activity (US Department of Homeland Security 2011).

The *Drink or Die* group produced and released a variety of pirated content, including copyrighted software, games, music, and digital videos. Members were widely dispersed in terrestrial space but networked in cyberspace. They included a relatively large proportion of university students who were technologically sophisticated and skilled in security, programming, and Internet communication. The group's activities entailed a division of labor. New content was often obtained through employees of software companies; "crackers" stripped the content of its electronic protection; "testers" made sure the unprotected version worked; and "packers" distributed the pirated version to around 10,000 publicly accessible sites around the Internet. The content was available to casual users and to other criminal enterprises for commercial distribution.

BOTNETS

Many law-abiding individuals have become unintentionally implicated in organized crime through botnets. When one's computer has been remotely commandeered and used in furtherance of criminal activity, an unwitting user is implicitly involved in organized criminal activity. It is usually more appropriate to regard them as victims, not criminals.

THE THREAT TO PRIVACY

Well over a century ago, long before the dawn of the digital age, the issue of individual privacy was the subject of a seminal article in the *Harvard Law Review* (Warren and Brandeis 1890). The junior author, Louis Brandeis, went on to become a famous justice of the US Supreme Court. One of the article's concerns related to the "unauthorized circulation of portraits of private persons" (p. 195). With uncanny prescience, they observed that "Instantaneous photographs and newspaper enterprise have invaded the sacred precincts of private and domestic life; and numerous mechanical devices threaten to make good the prediction that 'what is whispered in the closet shall be proclaimed from the housetops'" (p. 195). One hundred twenty-five years after these words were published, hundreds of private images of female celebrities were made available online, having been plucked from the cloud and distributed by hackers (Gibbs 2014).

Threats to privacy in the digital age emanate from three main sources: individual cybercriminals, commercial organizations, and governments. We have already seen how some criminals will engage in electronic voyeurism. Others will seek to steal personal financial information such as credit card and bank account details. Others, still, will intrude on your privacy by flooding your e-mail inbox with offers too good to be true. But violation of your privacy is by no means the monopoly of criminals.

Among the greatest threats to one's digital privacy are those posed by legitimate commercial entities (Grabosky, Smith, and Dempsey 2001, ch. 10). Most people leave their footprints all over cyberspace. Information about the websites you visit, the products you buy, and various other data such as your age and place of residence are scattered throughout cyberspace. Technologies of data-matching enable the compilation of electronic dossiers in considerable detail. These may be bought and sold for marketing purposes.

BE CAREFUL WHERE YOU VENTURE IN CYBERSPACE

In 1997, The Australian Minister for Justice contacted the Australian Institute of Criminology, where I was employed at the time, and asked for briefing notes on the subject of sex slavery. Illegal trafficking in persons, especially when it involved an element of coercion, had become one of substantial concern to the Australian Government. Although it was an issue about which I knew or cared little, I was assigned the task. My immediate strategy was to enter the term "sex slavery" on Google Advanced Search. Although this generated many hits, the vast majority was totally devoid of policy relevance. After further searching, I compiled a set of notes relating to the law of kidnapping and abduction in various jurisdictions, Australian and overseas, and forwarded them as requested. Relieved to be finished with the task at hand, I returned to more mundane matters. But my research came back to haunt me: Over the next month, I received a number of unsolicited e-mail advertisements of a very salacious nature. The moral of the story is that unless you take extraordinary steps to cover your tracks, you will leave footprints all over those corners of cyberspace where you venture.

Those readers who may be tempted to follow in my footsteps should know that my original research strategy now yields more policy-relevant content. For more on online privacy, see Grabosky, Smith, and Dempsey (2001), ch. 10.

At times, sensitive personal information may be disclosed by mistake. Data on patients of health systems have been inadvertently made public. Mass e-mailings may accidentally include the addresses of all intended recipients. Some people may be quite pleased that Amazon.com knows what books they buy. Others may not. A story is told about a telephone company that offered special discounts to customers who regularly call individual numbers. Legend has it that on one occasion, a housewife received a standard telephone bill, with just such an offer enclosed. In this case, the specified number was unfamiliar to her. Curiosity drove her to

ring the number, and she found that the subscriber was having an affair
with her husband.

As recent events have indicated, the state also poses a threat to personal privacy. Surveillance of citizens, by agents of government or by electronic means, has long been a technique employed by totalitarian
governments, symbolized by the expression "Big Brother Is Watching
You" (Orwell 1951). Suspicions that liberal democracies are also using
these methods have recently been confirmed.

The same technologies of data matching that permit the compilation of
electronic dossiers are available to governments no less than to commercial entities. A "Total Information Awareness Program" was developed by
the Defense Advanced Research Projects Agency (DARPA) to create a
grand centralized database ostensibly for the purpose of detecting terrorist activity. The name was subsequently changed to "Terrorism Information Awareness Program" (Electronic Privacy Information Center 2005).
Subsequent developments have been the subject of disclosures by Edward
Snowden (Greenwald 2014). Over a decade ago, a report by the (then)
General Accounting Office identified almost 200 data mining projects
either operational or in the planning stage, across the US federal government (US General Accounting Office 2004). The fact that much of this
was designed to improve customer service may be of no consolation, as
benign collections may have sinister applications: US Census data were
used to identify Japanese Americans for internment during World War II
(Seltzer and Anderson 2001).

Despite the existence of the Fourth Amendment to the US Constitution, and the exacting provisions of Title 18 US Code (which authorize
the interception of telecommunications under some circumstances, subject to judicial authorization), a citizen enjoys only a modicum of privacy.
The Internet is, of course, subject to surveillance. The FBI has deployed
network collection technologies (including one initially referred to as
"Carnivore") on numerous occasions. The name was changed to a less
threatening DCS 1000 (US Federal Bureau of Investigation 2003).

In the United States, the law allows the government easier access to
stored data than to data in transit. Messages stored on the server of
an Internet Service Provider are accessible pursuant to a subpoena,
rather than a warrant for interception. Well over a decade ago, America On
Line (AOL) was responding to over 1,000 criminal warrants per month

(Liptak 2006). Governments have begun to enact legislation to require retention of Internet data in order to enable retrospective access to data that were once short lived.

The aforementioned developments were but mere hints of what was to come. On December 16, 2005, the *New York Times* published an article reporting that President Bush secretly authorized surveillance on US citizens and residents without the warrants ordinarily required by law (Risen and Lichtblau 2005). The article had been withheld from publication for a year at the request of the White House. The Administration contended that it had legal authority consistent with the President's as Commander in Chief. The issue became a titanic struggle over competing objectives of privacy and security.

In January 2006 the US Department of Justice, in the course of preparing a justification for a controversial Internet pornography law, subpoenaed logs showing common search terms and a list of websites indexed by the Google's search engines. The request sought a "random sample of 1 million URLs" and "copies of the text of each search string entered onto Google's search engine over a 1-week period." Although the request did not seek the identity of individual users, the potential for future violations of privacy was not lost on the general public. All of this became boldly apparent in June 2013 with Edward Snowden's revelations of NSA surveillance.

A large-scale program of data capture, storage, and analysis had been undertaken since 2001 by the NSA. Outlined initially by Bamford (2008) with additional classified details subsequently disclosed by Edward Snowden, the program has relied extensively on the cooperation of private sector telecommunications carriers and service providers, and on the involvement of privately engaged consultants, of whom Snowden was one. Cooperating companies included Microsoft, Google, Yahoo!, Facebook, Pal Talk, You Tube, Skype, AOL, and Apple. The program reportedly captured and stored a wide range of data, including e-mail, chatroom exchanges, voice-over Internet protocol (VOIP), photos, stored data, file transfers, video conferencing, and other social network content (Gidda 2013; Greenwald and MacAskill 2013; Greenwald 2013). The NSA and its private sector partners have also succeeded in circumventing most online encryption technologies (Perlroth, Larson, and Scott 2013).

[7]

INVESTIGATION, PROSECUTION, AND SENTENCING

Cybercrime may come to the attention of the authorities after the fact or while in progress. In either case, it may not be apparent who the offender is or where he or she is physically situated. The challenge of attribution was noted in Chapter Three.

The initial indication of cybercrime is usually an attempt at unauthorized access. That is, someone is trying to get into a computer where the person should not be. When such an intrusion is first detected, it may not be apparent whether the intruder is a teenage adventurer, a technician working for an organized criminal group, or the intelligence service of a foreign state.

In the most inept cases of cybercrime, the offender will leave his or her tracks in numerous places. The offending communication will be traceable to an IP address, whose physical location will be obvious. Those more sophisticated offenders who impersonate other users, who "loop" and "weave" their communications across a number of jurisdictions, and conceal the content of their communications by encrypting them pose the more difficult challenges for law enforcement.

Cybercrime scenes can vary substantially as well. Crimes can be initiated from a workstation within a large organization or from the comfort of an offender's bedroom. The targets of cybercrime may be widely dispersed, as is the case with computer viruses, or very localized, as is the case with the computer of a victim of stalking. Evidence may be found at the physical location of the perpetrator, of the victim, or at numerous locations throughout cyberspace.

The nature of the investigation will depend on the preferences of the victim and the priorities of the investigator. These may not always coincide (Nhan 2010). As we have noted, many institutional victims, such as banks, may not wish the world to know that their systems have been successfully attacked. Their main concerns are in securing their systems (i.e., hardening the target) and recovering their losses, if possible. If the offender is an insider or a disgruntled former employee, this can, in some cases, be achieved without resort to prosecution. A veritable industry of private forensic computing specialists (many drawn from the ranks of former police with expertise in computer crime investigation) exists for this purpose. If the organization is dependent on IT for most of its business (especially the case with e-commerce), it is important that the system remain up and running as close to normal as possible.

Police, on the other hand, are primarily concerned with obtaining evidence sufficient to secure a conviction in a court of law. One can envisage circumstances in which the private interests of the victim may be in tension with what the police regard as the public interest. In situations such as these, who should prevail?

Digital evidence of a crime may be commingled with a great deal of other information, totally irrelevant to the investigation; the metaphor of the needle in the haystack is not entirely inappropriate. Even with automated search tools, finding that needle may be extremely difficult and time consuming.

In circumstances where the system itself was the instrument of the offence, seizure of the entire system may be an option. But such a course of action may cause undue inconvenience and considerable loss to innocent proprietors and their clients. In one case, *Steve Jackson Games, Inc. v. United States Secret Service* (1994) 36 F.3d 457 (5th Cir), the US government seized hardware and data files from a small Texas games manufacturer and Internet service provider. The disruption was severe and nearly put the company out of business. The material seized was thought to contain evidence of an offence by one of the company's customers. Neither the company nor its owner was ever prosecuted. Eventually, a federal court awarded damages to the company.

Nowadays, as we live in an increasingly networked environment, seizure of an entire system is not only unrealistic but also logistically impossible. A more appropriate option, where feasible, is to make two copies of the contents of a hard drive on which criminal evidence may be located. One can then be used for analysis and the other sealed and kept as a backup. Making only one copy enhances the risk of loss or damage. It is important to preserve the integrity of evidence, lest the accused challenge it in court.

Given the recent democratization of encryption technology, and its take-up by cybercriminals, a number of nations are moving toward compulsory disclosure of cryptographic keys subject to judicial oversight.

Authorities in the United States must go to greater lengths in order to obtain encryption keys because the Fifth Amendment to the US Constitution protects individuals against self-incrimination. The right to remain silent applies to the disclosure of encryption keys no less than to other potentially incriminating information. To compensate for this Constitutional impediment, US federal authorities have introduced legislation that would make it an offence to use encryption to conceal incriminating communication relating to a crime that they are committing or attempting to commit.

Those countries unconstrained by a bill of rights have devised a simpler solution to the challenge of encryption. They simply require individuals to disclose encryption keys or face criminal charges. In the United Kingdom, this can entail imprisonment for up to two years, in Australia, six months.[1] In Europe, Article 6 of the Rome Convention could be a barrier to such compulsory disclosure, although the European Commission on Human Rights has restricted the scope of the article to oral statements. Nevertheless, European procedures for compulsory decryption would have to be formulated precisely in order to withstand judicial scrutiny.

SEARCH AND SEIZURE

The American Revolution was fought, in part, because of the repressive practices of British colonial rule. Therefore, it is not surprising that the Constitution of the new United States guaranteed certain protections against governmental heavy-handedness. In the words of the Fourth Amendment, "The right of the people to be secure in their persons, houses,

MANAGING ENCRYPTED EVIDENCE

One case where investigators went to exceptional lengths to obtain an encryption key was the investigation of a member of a prominent organized crime family on the East Coast of the United States. The individual was under investigation for illegal gambling and loan sharking. A clandestine search of the subject's office revealed a computer, but investigators were unable to access an encrypted file in the computer that they suspected contained evidence of criminal activity.

The FBI obtained additional warrants, authorizing them to undertake another surreptitious entry and to install a device developed by FBI engineers known as a key logger system (KLS) on the subject's computer. This would record the password to the encrypted information. The KLS was configured so that it only operated when the computer was not connected to the Internet. This spared the investigators the necessity of obtaining a wiretap warrant (*United States v. Scarfo*, 180 F.Supp.2d 572 [D. N.J. 2001]).

The device worked as intended and the investigators successfully obtained access to the subject's encrypted file. Based on the evidence contained in the file, the government charged him with a number of offences.

The defense was unsuccessful in challenging the validity of the warrants and the accused pleaded guilty in February 2002 (Electronic Privacy Information Center 2003; *United States v. Scarfo*, 180 F. Supp.2d 572 [D. N.J. 2001]).

Nowadays, technologies of remote search are making devices such as the KLS largely obsolete.

papers, and effects, against unreasonable searches and seizures, shall not be violated, and no Warrants shall issue, but upon probable cause, supported by Oath or affirmation, and particularly describing the place to be searched, and the persons or things to be seized." The specificity of a warrant required under US law stands in stark contrast to the permissiveness of "general warrants" allowed by some other jurisdictions. These allow a degree of "rummaging" through a suspect's possessions on the off-chance that some incriminating evidence may turn up.

Long after the founding of the new republic, as technologies enabled the interception of communications between private citizens, protections against wiretapping and other forms of electronic eavesdropping were also introduced. Because of the particularly intrusive nature of telecommunications interception, requirements for a warrant are particularly stringent. Investigators ignore these constraints at their peril, for failure to comply with the law can result in an offender going free; in extreme cases, it can result in criminal charges being laid against the investigator.

Procedural issues relating to the investigation of cybercrime may be considered on three dimensions: the nature of the investigative measure(s) to be used, the legal requirements for its use, and the office or institution ultimately authorizing the activity in question. Ideally, each of these will vary depending upon the apparent severity of the alleged offence.

Basic investigative measures vary in intrusiveness. In ascending order, they can include the following:

- Orders to Internet service providers (ISPs) or other service providers for preservation of data
- Orders to relinquish data on individual subscribers or traffic
- Orders to relinquish stored content data
- Real-time collection of stored content data
- Real-time collection of content data in transit
- Search and/or seizure of a suspect's files or hardware

Legal standards, where they exist, will vary in rigor. At a minimum, some evidence of a criminal act will be necessary. More intrusive methods may require evidence of a relatively serious crime and probable cause that the suspect has committed the alleged offence. Finally, use of a specific investigative method may be subject to the authorization of a public official, to ensure that the proposed techniques are consistent with the standards of justification. Authorization for the use of a particular measure may be made by law enforcement, prosecutors, judicial authorities, or other designated officials.

In some cases, evidence may be obtainable in publicly accessible locations. To this end, law enforcement agencies have designed elaborate ruses to trap computer criminals. In a 1995 operation code-named "Operation Cybersnare," the US Secret Service covertly established an Internet discussion group that served as a forum for the purchase of stolen cellular phone access numbers, credit card numbers, and personal identity information. Criminals joining the group who offered illicit products for sale were identified and prosecuted (Gold 1995). The requirement in many jurisdictions that a search warrant be based on *probable cause* is intended to protect citizens from "fishing expeditions" or vindictive intrusions. With regard to the search and seizure of digital evidence, probable cause may be established by an Internet protocol (IP) address indicating the computer from which the crime may have originated. An IP address may be available from the victim or from a service provider; the ISP may then be requested or compelled to provide the name and physical address of the suspect. Probable cause may also be based on information relating to online e-mail accounts or accounts with websites trading in contraband (*R. v. Spencer*, 2014 SCC 43 [2014] 2 S.C.R. 212).

UNDERCOVER INVESTIGATIONS

The practice of law enforcement officers posing online as children in order to trap adults in search of illicit assignations has occurred for over a decade and is common in many Western democracies (Smith et al 2004, p. 190; Krone 2005b; Urbas 2010). Other countries do not permit online investigations, regarding them as an excessive use of police power. Undercover patrolling of the Internet can encroach upon personal privacy and can inhibit freedom of expression, not only of criminals but of innocent persons as well.

Undercover investigations of cybercrime take two basic forms. In the first, a law enforcement agent will seek to establish trust within a cybercriminal community, to obtain intelligence, to observe criminal activity as it occurs, or to collect evidence. The establishment of trust is facilitated by the anonymity apparently afforded by the Internet.

This type of law enforcement work is extremely labor intensive, as trust is rarely established instantly. The building of trust may require many months of dependable interactions with the targets of investigation. Since much cybercrime activity is not limited to conventional business hours, the undercover cybercrime investigator's task may be all the more difficult. A celebrated example of this type of investigation involved the malware bazaar known as Dark Market. An undercover FBI agent was able to ingratiate himself, and he became an indispensable administrator of the marketplace (Glenny 2011).

In 2010, the FBI actually established an undercover carding forum called "Carder Profit," which recruited and "registered" a number of individuals, whose communications with other "members" were recorded by agents. Among the products allegedly offered for sale were remote access tools, keystroke loggers, and credit card details. Registrants were required to provide valid e-mail addresses, which, along with IP addresses of users, were duly noted by investigators. To ensure that the merely naïve or curious were not caught up in the sting, which led to twenty-four arrests in eight countries around the world, potential recruits had to be nominated by two registered members (FBI 2012).

Another basic strategy of cybercrime investigation is to engage a cybercriminal to work on behalf of law enforcement. This is more easily arranged when the offender has been apprehended for an offence. Standard practice is to offer the offender a degree of leniency in return for his or her assistance in identifying other criminals and/or in collecting evidence for use against them. Hector Monsegur, one of the more prominent participants in the Anonymous and LulzSec groups, was arrested by the FBI and agreed to assist its agents with further investigations. The information that Monsegur provided led to the arrests of eight alleged offenders, and his cooperation with prosecutors was said to result in the disruption of at least 300 cyberattacks. Under normal circumstances, the offences with which Monsegur had been charged would result in a sentence of approximately twenty-one to twenty-six years. The prosecutor requested that the judge impose a substantially lower sentence, which she did. She complimented Monsegur and sentenced him to time served, taking into consideration seven months that he spent in custody awaiting disposition (Weiser 2014). The fact that Monsegur also assisted the government in a campaign of cyberattacks on foreign websites may also have been to his advantage (Mazzetti 2014).

The issue of trust is also central to the relationship between law enforcement agents and the offenders whom they recruit to work with them. There is always a risk that despite their apparent cooperation, an accused may continue her criminal activity over the course of assisting in a police investigation. This can result in continuing victimization and increasing losses to victims. One of the more reckless of these cybercriminals was Albert Gonzalez. A principal of Shadowcrew, an online marketplace for stolen credit card details, Gonzalez was charged with the large-scale theft of credit card details and with ATM fraud. Arrested by the US Secret Service, he was convicted and given a lenient sentence in return for his assistance in investigating other cybercrimes. After a time as a valued and trusted Secret Service informer, Gonzalez resumed his own criminal activities, until he was again caught. Alleged on this occasion to have stolen some 130 million credit card numbers, he was convicted and sentenced to twenty years of imprisonment (Verini 2010).

The aforementioned examples suggest that cybercrime investigations often involve the building (and subsequent betrayal) of trust in undercover agents or the manufacture of mistrust among cybercriminals by law enforcement. Conversely, the development and reassurance of trust remains one of the most significant challenges faced by cybercriminals (Décary-Hétu and Dupont 2012).

An additional risk of undercover cyberpolicing is that the undercover officer(s) or agent(s) will induce a suspect to engage in criminal activity that would not otherwise occur. The problem here is that in some jurisdictions, most notably in the United States, the absence of a predisposition to create a crime will allow a defense of entrapment. The undercover investigator must therefore take great pains not to initiate a crime.

COLLECTING, PRESERVING, ANALYZING, AND PRESENTING DIGITAL EVIDENCE

One of the most significant differences between cybercrime and terrestrial crime is the nature of evidence. There are differences in the form it takes, how it is stored, where it is located, how it is found, and in the physical limitations of what it will tell you. Digital evidence is intangible. It is often volatile, in that it may no longer be accessible after a brief period. And it may also be massive in quantity, thereby posing substantial logistical challenges.

Nevertheless, the basic principles remain the same for handling digital evidence as for physical evidence (McKemmish 1999). The seizure of hardware or of digital content should be no more intrusive than necessary. The exponential increase in storage capacity that has been evident since the widespread take-up of digital technology makes the inspection of massive volumes of digital information extraordinarily time consuming. Accordingly, it may be preferable to conduct a search off-site. In such cases, it is possible to produce an identical copy of the suspect hard drive (called an "image copy") and remove it to a forensic laboratory for analysis. Ideally, examination of the evidence will entail no alteration or modification of the data. The original data would be preserved and copied; and any examination would be carried out on the copy. Any changes to the original, if necessary, should be explicitly documented and justified, in order to minimize defense challenges to its integrity. In court, the evidence should be presented in a manner that does not change its meaning. The standard text on digital evidence is the work of Casey (2011); a variety of products are in use around the world that enable perfect imaging of digital content, whether it exists on a hard drive, peripherals, or a mobile phone.

There are three basic issues arising from the use of electronic evidence. First, the defense may question the identity of the author of the evidence in question ("It wasn't me; it was somebody else"). Second, the defense can claim that the evidence was tampered with. Third, it can argue that the unreliability of computer programs created inaccuracies in the output.

Efforts to standardize forensic procedures have occurred on a number of fronts. The Computer Crime and Intellectual Property Section of the US Department of Justice developed *Federal Guidelines for Searching and Seizing Computers* in 1994. The guidelines have been revised and updated periodically since then, most recently under the title *Searching and Seizing Computers and Obtaining Electronic Evidence in Criminal Investigations* (US Department of Justice 2014a).

Standardized forensic procedures have also been developed by the FBI's Computer Analysis Response Team (CART) created in 1992 to manage issues arising from the increasing number of investigations involving digital technology. In the United States, courts have given their imprimatur to certain standardized forensic practices. An early example of best practice in search and seizure of computer evidence was provided in *United States v. Triumph Capital Group et al.* (211 F.R.D. 31 [D. Conn. 2002]). There the defense moved to suppress evidence in a public corruption case that was seized from a laptop computer. The judgment described in great detail the steps taken at each stage of the search; it was, and remains, a textbook lesson in computer forensics. Detailed guidelines for the examination of digital evidence have been set out in a number of countries, such as the United States (US Department of Justice 2004d). In the United Kingdom, the Association of Chief Police Officers (2012) has drafted guidelines in relation to preferred forensic procedures.

This developing standardization of forensic practice (assuming that investigators adhere to these standards) will give the defense less opportunity to challenge investigative techniques. Prosecutors should be aware that departures from recognized best practices, to the extent that they occur, are likely to be seized upon by defense counsel. In addition, the laws of evidence in a given jurisdiction should be able to accommodate the transformation of intangible evidence into a form intelligible to judges and juries.

One of the most important policy decisions relating to digital evidence relates to the extent to which telecommunications carriers and service providers may be required to assist law enforcement. In most developed nations, telecommunications infrastructure is privately owned, but subject to government regulation and license. More than two decades ago, the US Congress enacted the Communications Assistance for Law Enforcement Act (CALEA), requiring telecommunications carriers and equipment manufacturers to configure their systems in a manner that would allow federal agencies to intercept telephone traffic. The law has since been amended to include Internet communication. In addition to enhanced interception capabilities, the government has also sought to require ISPs to retain data for an extended period, in order to allow law enforcement agencies to access these data for investigative purposes. The industry has a financial interest in retaining some information, such as transaction information (who contacted whom, when, and for how long) for billing purposes. But indefinite retention of digital information requires storage space, and storage costs money.

In addition, many Internet users value their privacy and would be most uncomfortable to learn that ISPs may (willingly or pursuant to legal order) disclose their online activity with the government. ISPs who are seen to favor government preferences over those of their customers may find themselves in a difficult position.

Precisely what financial burdens private industry should be required to bear in order to assist law enforcement is an important policy question. There is no simple answer, for the imposition of significant costs on industry may detract from profitability, which may in turn inhibit the growth of information technology and the economic development on which it will depend.

THE GLOBAL ARENA OF CYBERCRIME INVESTIGATION

The challenge of investigating and prosecuting cybercrime when it occurs in one's own jurisdiction is daunting enough. When a cybercrime originates on the other side of the world, the problems are compounded.

First is the challenge of finding out where the offence originates. To conceal their location, cybercriminals physically present in one jurisdiction may "loop" or "weave" their attacks through a number of jurisdictions on the way to their target. Even in the absence of deliberate intent to conceal one's location, the nature of Internet traffic is such that criminal communications may cross jurisdictional boundaries as a matter of course. In one case involving the stalking of a woman in Hong Kong, investigators traced the offensive communication to a server in Colorado. Inquiries in Colorado revealed that the communication had originated in Hong Kong.

As we have seen, the identity of the offender and the nature of the offence may not be immediately apparent to either the victim or to the investigator. An attempted intrusion may be the first step in a chain of successive crimes, and it may be the work of a teenage hacker, an organized crime group, or agents of a foreign government. Once it is determined that a computer crime has originated from a foreign jurisdiction, the cooperation of authorities in that jurisdiction must be sought in order to identify the suspect. This may be difficult, since authorities in other countries may lack the capacity to assist. They may simply not have officers with sufficient training in computer forensics to be of much help. A recent report by the United Nations Office on Drugs and Crime (UNODC 2013) concluded that many countries lack the technical capacity or legal framework to enable effective investigation of cybercrime. Accordingly, many countries would require foreign technical assistance in order to contribute to cross border investigations. They may also lack interest; their priorities may simply lie elsewhere. It has been suggested that authorities in Russia are tolerant of cybercrime committed from within its borders, as long as it is directed at foreign targets.

The fact that an offence (or elements of an offence) occurred on foreign soil raises complex questions, since issues of national sovereignty are at stake. For example, police officials from the People's Republic of China may not simply get on an airplane, fly to the United States, and execute a search on a computer located at the residence of a Falun Gong supporter in Los Angeles. Of course, technologies now exist that enable searches to be executed remotely, using many of the same methods as hackers. One of the murky areas of the law of cybercriminal procedure relates to the legal authority that is required in order to conduct such searches across national frontiers.

In cases where mutual assistance arrangements are weak or nonexistent, authorities may go to great lengths to lay their hands on a suspect and obtain incriminating evidence. In the 1990s two residents of Chelyabinsk, Russia, Alexey Ivanov and Vasiliy Gorshkov, exploited a weakness in Windows NT and launched a number of intrusions against Internet service providers, online banks, and e-commerce sites in the United States. The offenders succeeded in stealing over 56,000 credit card numbers and other personal financial information of the sites' customers. They then sought to extort money from the victims by threatening to publish customers' data and damage the companies' computers. They manipulated e-Bay auctions by using anonymous e-mail accounts to be both seller and winning bidder in the one auction. The online payments system PayPal was also defrauded by using cash generated from stolen credit cards to pay for various products.

The suspects were resident in Russia, and Russian authorities were disinclined to cooperate with their US counterparts. To overcome this substantial impediment, FBI agents executed an undercover operation. Posing as representatives of a security firm called "Invita," the agents made contact with Gorshkov and Ivanov in mid-2000, ostensibly to discuss employment opportunities in the United States. At the invitation of the agents, the two Russians demonstrated their hacking skills from Russia against a test network that had been established for the purpose. They were then invited to Seattle with the prospects of employment.

The two flew to Seattle, all expenses paid, and were "interviewed" about their computing skills. In the course of their presentation, Gorshkov accessed his computer system back in Russia. The interview took place in offices that were well equipped—with CCTV and with other technologies that enabled the FBI to record their interviewees' keystrokes. The two were then arrested and charged with a spate of offences, including fraud, extortion, and unauthorized computer intrusions. To strengthen their case, FBI investigators downloaded additional incriminating evidence remotely from Gorshkov's computer in Russia. Russian authorities were not pleased, regarding this remote search as a violation of national sovereignty (Schroeder 2012).

Traditionally, obtaining cooperation from a foreign law enforcement agency required a formal and laborious process. Substantial documentation took time to prepare and delays could arise in obtaining official signatures. Today, the volatility of much electronic evidence and the speed with which cybercrime can be committed from one side of the world against a target on the other makes speedy cooperation in real time highly desirable. To this end, a group of technologically advanced nations have developed a 24/7 network of contacts to provide a platform for mutual assistance in transnational cybercrime cases.

JURISDICTION

Given the "borderless" nature of cybercrime, offences are often committed from one jurisdiction ("Country A") against a target in another nation ("Country B"), after having been routed through servers in one or more intermediate countries ("Countries C, D, E...."). This raises the question of where the crime occurred and which country might be responsible for investigating and prosecuting the case. If an offender is identified and apprehended, it may be difficult or impossible to hand him or her over to a requesting country, since cooperation between jurisdictions is not always automatic.

Sovereign states may choose to assert jurisdiction over a cybercrime according to any of a number of principles. The principle of *territoriality* holds that a state can prosecute if a crime, or if any element of a crime, occurs within its territorial boundaries. Thus, the United States prosecuted a British subject resident in Australia for his involvement in the

US-based Drink or Die digital piracy ring, even though he had never set foot in the United States before he was extradited there to face trial. According to the principle of *effects*, a state can establish jurisdiction of criminal activity, wherever it occurs, that produces substantial effects on its own territory. Alleged cyberattacks on US government and business sites by officers of the Peoples Liberation Army, noted earlier, gave rise to criminal charges in 2014. Under the principle of *nationality*, a state can prosecute its own citizens or habitual residents for crimes committed anywhere; or it can prosecute foreign nationals for crimes committed against its citizens abroad. The *protective* principle provides the basis for prosecuting crimes committed abroad that threaten one's own national security. The principle of *universality* covers the prosecution of special crimes such as war crimes, maritime piracy, or crimes against humanity, wherever they may have occurred. Malaysia claims jurisdiction over cybercrimes committed anywhere on the planet, as long as they correspond to comparable offences under Malaysian law.

Some countries will not extradite their own citizens under any circumstances. Others will not extradite a suspect if he or she is liable to face execution in the event of conviction. Under these circumstances, the requesting country will be required to make an undertaking not to impose the death penalty. Few, if any, countries will extradite a juvenile. "Mafia Boy," the fifteen-year-old who was responsible for the denial of service attacks against major e-retailers in 2000, was prosecuted by Canadian authorities instead.

Extradition is most easily achieved pursuant to formal agreements between countries. These usually require what is termed "dual criminality"; that is, the offence in question must be against the law in both the country requesting extradition and in the country where he or she may be located. Onel de Guzman, who released the "I Love You" virus, could not be extradited to the United States because what he did was not, at that time, an offense under Philippine law. Conversely, offensive political speech (such as neo-Nazi propaganda) that originates in the United States cannot give rise to international mutual assistance or extradition, since it is protected by the First Amendment to the US Constitution. A 2013 UNODC report noted that only a relatively small number of countries make it a crime to create, possess, or distribute computer misuse technologies such as malware and hacker tools. An offender may thus operate with impunity as long as he or she remains in the jurisdiction where the act in question is not covered by the substantive criminal law.

Extradition agreements usually require that the crime in question must be of a sufficient degree of severity, usually one requiring a term of imprisonment. This is understandable, given the time and expense involved in adjudicating the extradition request and transporting the suspect to the requesting country. Obviously, it is also essential that the evidence against the accused is sufficient to justify prosecution.

In the case of the two extortionists, Gorshkov and Ivanov, US authorities were aware that Russian assistance in investigation and eventual extradition was most unlikely. The remote search of computers situated on Russian soil caused Russian authorities great concern, to the extent that one of the FBI investigators was charged in absentia with a crime under Russian law.

The Citibank hacker, Vladimir Levin, made the mistake of leaving Russia to attend a trade show in the United Kingdom. UK authorities had no reservations about cooperating with their counterparts in the United States. When they identified Levin from a watch list at Heathrow Airport, they took him into custody. Having determined that what he was alleged to have done was in fact covered by UK law, they extradited him to the United States, where he was tried and convicted.

CLOUD COMPUTING

The nature of digital technology is such that issues of jurisdiction are complicated still further. "Cloud computing" is a term that refers to the remote storage of data, operating systems, and application services, which may then be shared by a number of parties under multi-tenancy arrangements. The concept dates from the early days of computing, dominated as it was by mainframes; online e-mail systems, among the more common examples, are now three decades old. The popularity of cloud computing in recent years is due to the significant cost savings that can be realized through the sharing of resources and the wider distribution of infrastructure costs. Although the origin of the term has been traced to executives of Compaq Computer in 1996, cloud computing, and the architecture that it describes, became popular a decade later when used by Amazon to

FOREIGN PROSECUTION

A cybercrime committed from Country A to Country B, assuming a suspect has been identified and the behavior in question violated the laws of both countries, raises the question of who will prosecute. Perhaps the easiest solution is to leave the matter to authorities in the country from which the perpetrator undertook the alleged criminal activity. It is a much less costly and time-consuming path to take than extradition. One example of the host country prosecuting a transnational offender was the case of an individual in Melbourne, Australia, who sent over three million e-mail messages to addressees in Australia and the United States with a view toward manipulating the price of shares in a company traded on the NASDAQ exchange in New York. He timed his own trades in the company's shares appropriately and pocketed a profit of around $15,000. In cases of this nature, it is common for the US Securities and Exchange Commission to seek disgorgement of the ill-gotten gains and an injunction on the perpetrator not to reoffend. Rather than mobilize the federal criminal process and seek to extradite the offender, US authorities were happy to leave prosecution to Australia. The accused pleaded guilty, was sentenced to prison for three years, and was released on probation after three months, subject to good behavior.[2]

refer to files, software, and computer power that were accessible over the Web instead of individual desktop workstations (Regalado 2011). The distributed nature of the "cloud" raises the question of precisely where, in jurisdictional terms, data in the cloud may be deemed to exist. In other words, if evidence of an alleged crime exists in a cloud, potentially dispersed over a number of jurisdictions, from whom does one seek authority to conduct a search (Martini and Choo 2015)?

Despite the challenges posed by the transnational nature of much cybercrime, there have been some stunning examples of success in the investigation and prosecution of offences committed by participants in cross-national criminal conspiracies. Coordination is crucial to the interdiction of many criminal conspiracies, because a raid on one conspirator alone can indicate to other participants that law enforcement may be on their trail, and it may inspire them to destroy incriminating evidence. The following are but a few examples of successful coordinated investigations.

OPERATION CATHEDRAL

In the mid-1990s, a California woman's complaint that her daughter had been molested by the father of one of the girl's friends led to an international child pornography ring that convened in an Internet chat room. In the course of the investigation, an encryption key was discovered that led to an even larger ring, whose members used sophisticated encryption technology and who rotated the location of the host server in order to avoid detection. The investigation led to arrests of members in twelve different countries.

OPERATION BUCCANEER

After a fourteen-month undercover operation, sixty-five searches were conducted in the United States and six foreign countries on December 11, 2001, against participants in the *Drink or Die* copyright piracy conspiracy. Three British defendants were sentenced to terms of imprisonment of eighteen months, two years, and two and a half years, respectively. US courts were more severe, imposing prison terms of forty-six, forty-one, and thirty-three months. The US government sought extradition of an alleged conspirator resident in Australia, who, for obvious reasons, tenaciously challenged the application up to and including an unsuccessful appeal to the High Court of Australia (US Department of Justice 2005e; *Griffiths v. United States of America & Anor* [2005] HCATrans 666 [2 September 2005]).

OPERATION ARTUS

At the end of 2001, German police executed a search warrant on a citizen suspected of offences related to child pornography. It became apparent that the suspect had been exchanging incriminating material over an Internet relay chat (IRC) channel. He subsequently provided police with the nicknames of some of his correspondents. The investigation led to the execution of seven search warrants in the United States and thirty simultaneous searches in ten foreign countries.

OPERATION FALCON

Operation Falcon identified a company that provided credit card support services to sites in Belarus (a former republic of the USSR) that offered online child pornography on a commercial basis. The company, Regpay, Inc., allegedly processed nearly $3 million in subscription fees (Ashcroft 2004). By accessing transaction details of the company's customers, in cooperation with French, Spanish, and Belarusian authorities, US investigators were able to identify suspected consumers of child pornography around the world. These leads were shared with law enforcement agencies in these suspects' home countries.

No fewer than 1,700 of these credit card transactions were referred to the Australian High Tech Crime Centre (AHTCC) leading to the identification in that country alone of over 700 potential suspects and the execution of more than 450 search warrants. According to the Commissioner of the Australian Federal Police, charges were laid against over 200 Australians (Keelty 2004).

OPERATION DELEGO

The *Dreamboard* child pornography ring was closed down by a multinational police investigation begun in 2009. The operation resulted in charges against seventy-two people in fourteen countries across five continents. Servers were situated in the United States, and the group's top administrators were located in France and Canada. Rules of conduct on the site's bulletin board were printed in English, Russian, Japanese, and Spanish. The investigation involved authorities from fourteen different nations: Canada, Denmark, Ecuador, France, Germany, Hungary, Kenya, the Netherlands, the Philippines, Qatar, Serbia, Sweden, Switzerland, and the United States. Three *Dreamboard* members were sentenced to life imprisonment. Forty-eight others received sentences averaging twenty years (US Department of Homeland Security, 2011; US Department of Justice, n.d.).

SILK ROAD

Silk Road was an online marketplace on the TOR underground network that afforded anonymity to buyers and sellers. This hidden service provided a forum for the purchase of illicit drugs, using bit-coins as the medium of exchange. Silk Road was shut down in October 2013, when its administrator Ross William Ulbricht (aka Dead Pirate Roberts) was arrested in San Francisco. Shortly thereafter, a number of Ulbricht's associates relaunched the site, but this too fell victim to interdiction by law enforcement. Ulbricht was sentenced to life imprisonment in 2015

In November 2014, more than 400 website addresses and computer servers hosting Silk Road 2.0 and other illicit marketplaces were seized in a coordinated law enforcement action. Operation Onymous involved police from seventeen nations, including Bulgaria, Czech Republic, Finland, France, Germany, Hungary, Ireland, Latvia, Lithuania, Luxembourg, Netherlands, Romania, Spain, Sweden, Switzerland, and the United Kingdom and the United States. The websites hosted dozens of "dark market" websites on the TOR network, where a variety of contraband products and illicit services were available for purchase (US Department of Justice 2014b, 2014c).

International cooperation may be difficult, if not impossible, under some circumstances. However, a convergence of interests between otherwise uncooperative states may produce surprising results. Relations between Taiwan and mainland China have traditionally been strained. Cooperation in the area of cybercrime control has been particularly difficult, since cyberattacks in both directions across the Taiwan Strait (some under government auspices) have been common (Chang 2012). Despite these impediments, a joint operation by the two jurisdictions in 2010 against a multinational fraud organization resulted in some 600 arrests across Southeast Asia (Wines 2011). From 2004 to 2010, Chinese police assisted forty-one countries in the investigation of 721 cybercrime cases (Chan and Wang 2015). Such cooperation would not have been possible in matters relating to cyber espionage, where state interests may be in conflict.

PROSECUTING CYBERCRIME

Only in recent decades has evidence in criminal cases existed in digital form. Assembling and preserving this evidence, and presenting it in court, requires familiarity with digital forensics that may not come naturally to prosecutors, particularly those who were born before the digital age. In the United States, every federal prosecutor's office has a member who has been designated as a computer hacking and intellectual property (CHIP) attorney. They have received extensive training in computer crime matters and bear primary responsibility for assisting their colleagues in such cases. This level of expertise is unusual, however, and usually lacking in smaller jurisdictions, particularly those countries on the other side of the digital divide.

Challenges faced by prosecutors in confronting cybercrime are in many other respects similar to those faced in dealing with conventional crime. To the extent that they become involved in the planning and conduct of investigations (as is often the case in the United States), they must ensure that the investigative practices to be employed are consistent with applicable constitutional safeguards and established analytical protocols.

When presented with a case, prosecutors must decide whether evidence is sufficient to sustain a conviction. Most prosecutors have more business than they can handle, and they must manage their resources to get the "biggest bang for the buck." In the United States, where the heads of most local prosecutors' offices are elected officials, career considerations, such a re-election as District Attorney or election to higher political office, may also be important. As such, prosecutors may be inclined to pursue high-profile murder cases rather than complex frauds, or arcane high-tech crimes.

In the English-speaking world at least, most computer crime cases are disposed of by a guilty plea. This is usually because prosecutors pursue matters where the evidence against the accused is overwhelming and the prospects of acquittal by a jury are remote. In such cases, the prospect of a lesser sentence following a plea of guilty is sufficient to persuade the defense to take that option.

In some cases, however, an accused will take his or her chances with a jury. In 1993, a student at the University of Edinburgh was charged with unauthorized access to computer systems. This he did not dispute. His defense was based on the claim that he was addicted to computers. Obsession with computers is by no means unheard of; a Center for Online and Internet Addiction was founded as early as 1995.[3] In this case, the judge instructed the jury that mere addiction did not negate intent, but the jury voted nevertheless to acquit. Despite this initial success, defenses based on addiction are not often run. After all, drug addiction is no defense to charges of burglary. Rather, the defense will raise the matter of diminished capacity resulting from addiction in seeking a reduced sentence.

The fact that evidence of a crime has been found on a computer is not ipso facto evidence of an accused's guilt. The defense, after all, can suggest that someone else may have had access to the computer in question. In order to prove that a particular individual had in fact committed the crime, it might be necessary to show that he or she was logged on to the computer at the time, or that he or she logged into an e-mail or bank account shortly thereafter.

When a defendant facing very serious charges is confronted with a strong prosecution case and the prospects of a long prison term if convicted, he or she may be more inclined to go for broke. Such was the choice of an eighth-grade math teacher in Albany, Georgia, who set up a website advertising photos of young girls. A police search of his computer revealed an abundance of incriminating evidence, and the defense made a desperate case. Counsel contended that the accused was a vigilante who was working undercover to expose Internet predators and child pornographers. It was further argued that his computer was hacked by a "Trojan Horse virus." His defense failed, and he was sentenced to seventeen and a half years in prison[4]

The Trojan Horse defense has met with greater success in the United Kingdom (Brenner, Carrier, and Henninger 2004). One teenager from Shaftesbury, Dorset, was acquitted of charges arising from an alleged Distributed Denial of Service attack that froze computers serving the port of Houston, Texas. Although a forensic examination of the defendant's computer revealed hacker tools but no evidence of a Trojan infection, the jury voted to acquit. Another UK case never got to court when the accused, charged with possessing child pornography, was actually found to have had a Trojan program on his computer. Prosecutors concluded that they had insufficient evidence to establish guilt beyond reasonable doubt and dismissed the charges. A routine virus check at the outset of an investigation seems a useful strategy to preempt problems of this nature.

The Trojan Horse defense is not an insurmountable challenge for prosecutors, as the successful prosecution of the Georgia math teacher has shown. What is required, for this, as for many ordinary cases, is complementary evidence consistent with guilt, ideally from a number of independent sources. The defendant's own level of computer literacy is one important factor. A person who is knowledgeable about computers and computer security should be less vulnerable to a Trojan infection than is a naïve user. The existence of firewalls and current antivirus software on a suspect's computer makes a Trojan defense less credible.

Additional weight could be provided by evidence of the defendant's knowledge and intent. In child pornography cases, this could include a very large collection of images, stored in a variety of formats, a history of visiting chat rooms where such images are traded, other indicia of an interest in such material, or communication with known pedophiles. Finally, thorough forensic analysis of the suspect's computer is also essential, including definitive steps to determine the presence or absence of "malware" and, if found, to identify its capabilities. As jurors became more familiar with digital technology, the mystique of the Trojan defense has tended to dissipate, and it has become a decreasingly successful defense tactic. Meanwhile, careful forensic procedures have hastened this demise.

Another defense that has been run in extreme cases is the so-called fantasy defense, most common in prosecutions arising from alleged attempts to lure children for illicit purposes. Typically, the defendant will claim that his or her actions were expressions of fantasy and not indicative of real intentions. One defendant was charged in 1999 with traveling from Seattle to Santa Monica for the purpose of meeting a person who had identified herself as a thirteen-year-old girl. (The "girl" turned out to be an FBI agent.) The defendant argued that almost everyone in chat rooms engages in what he called real-time fiction, or role playing, and that the person he would meet in Santa Monica could just as easily have been a forty-year-old woman. His travel to Santa Monica, therefore, was not for the purpose of committing a crime. After four days of deliberation, the jury was unable to reach a verdict. All but one of the men on the jury accepted the fantasy defense, while the six women did not. Pessimistic about the prospects of a fantasy defense in a retrial, he pleaded guilty to interstate travel with intent to engage in criminal sexual activity and received a relatively lenient sentence of nine months of in-home detention, five years of probation, and a fine of $20,000 (Smith, Grabosky, and Urbas 2004, p. 190).

EXEMPLARY PROSECUTIONS

Among the strategies of governmental response to cybercrime have been exemplary prosecutions, often coupled with stern warnings not to follow in the footsteps of the targeted offender. Such firm utterances are characteristic of prosecutors generally, but in the early years of cybercrime, they have been particularly noticeable. Their purpose is to counteract the ambivalence with which many people view certain types of cybercrime, especially hacking and piracy.

Following the arrest of an Israeli hacker charged with a series of intrusions into US military information systems, the Attorney General of the United States at the time, Janet Reno said, "This arrest should send a message to would-be computer hackers all over the world that the United States will treat computer intrusions as serious crimes. We will work around the world and in the depths of cyberspace to investigate and prosecute those who attack computer networks" (US Department of Justice 1998). Words such as "We will find them and bring them to justice" are familiar elements of the prosecutor's vocabulary.

SENTENCING

Determining an appropriate penalty to impose on a convicted cybercriminal can be a challenge. The aims of punishment are numerous, sometimes contradictory, and hardly embraced by everyone. They include the following:

- Deterrence (both of the convicted offender and those who might be tempted to follow in his or her footsteps)
- Rehabilitation of the offender
- Denunciation of the crime in question
- Retribution (exacting vengeance against the offender)
- Incapacitation of the offender
- Restitution or compensation to the victim of crime
- Reconciliation and reintegration of the offender

In addition to choosing a punishment that meets one or more of these objectives, a sentencing authority usually seeks to ensure that a penalty is *proportionate*—that it reflects the circumstances of a crime, and that it is *appropriate to the background of the offender.* One could be forgiven for suggesting that this is often a "mission impossible."

Those cybercriminals who are unfortunate enough to get convicted in a court of law will receive a sentence of some kind. The nature and severity of a sentence will vary from one jurisdiction to another, depending on the perceived heinousness of the offence and the background of the offender. There have been no large-scale systematic analyses of cyber sentencing. A small study conducted by Smith et al. (2004) reported that cyber sentences appear to be no more or less severe than those imposed on similarly situated terrestrial offenders. The two types of cybercrime that are met with the stiffest sentences in the United States are offences relating to child pornography and offences relating to large-scale theft of credit card details. Organized theft or piracy of intellectual property can also attract a harsh response. In the United States, those who commit the most egregious cases of Internet child pornography have received life sentences. Less heinous child image offenses received sentences of just under twenty years of imprisonment. Major cases of credit card fraud can also attract sentences of twenty years. The more serious software piracy cases have tended to receive prison sentences of approximately five years.

In the United States, apparent disparities in sentences imposed by federal judges led to the creation of the US Sentencing Commission in 1984. At issue was the principle that similar crimes, committed by similar offenders, should receive similar punishments. Within the statutory maximum and minimum sentences prescribed by Congress for each federal offence, the Sentencing Commission developed a set of guidelines to inform judicial discretion. Upward and downward departures within these guidelines could occur, depending upon the presence or absence of aggravating or mitigating circumstances, respectively.

The sentencing guidelines have always been controversial. Federal judges, in particular, were concerned that their sentencing discretion was severely limited. The status of the guidelines has changed in light of subsequent litigation. In *United States v. Booker* (2005), the US Supreme Court held that facts (such as the amount of drugs involved in a sale) that might serve as the basis for an increased sentence under the guidelines must be determined by a jury, and that the Guidelines could no longer be mandatory, but rather only advisory.

What is important for the sentencing of cybercriminals is what the guidelines refer to as a "special skills enhancement." That is, an offender who uses special skills (such as those of a pilot, accountant, or chemist) that significantly facilitate the commission or the concealment of an offence may receive an increased sentence as a result. In the early years of the digital age, the digital divide between "tech-savvy" computer jocks and computer illiterates raised the question, just what constitutes the use of special skills in the commission of a cybercrime?

One offender had no formal computer training but was sufficiently skilled to gain unauthorized access to the computers of Pacific Bell to facilitate intercepting and seizing the telephone lines of a radio station. Two of his accomplices had discovered a computer program that could be used to "rig" the results of radio station promotional contests to ensure that they were the correct caller to win various prizes. Using this information, the offender called the radio station and "won" a $10,000 cash prize. The accomplices "won" at least two Porsche automobiles, a $20,000 cash prize, a $10,000 cash prize, and two trips to Hawaii. In addition, the offender was able to break into other sophisticated computer systems, place wiretaps on phones, and transfer large sums of money between banks. Although the Sentencing Guidelines provided that special skills "usually" require substantial education, training, or licensing, the offender received a special skills enhancement for his efforts because the skills in question were of a high level and not possessed by members of the general public (*United States v. Petersen* 98 F.3d 502 [9th Cir. 1996]).

In another illustration of special skills in furtherance of cybercrime, the accused hacked into a company's computer network and illegally installed a secure shell account that gave him continuing remote access. He used the system to store hacking programs and other information, and also installed a "sniffer" program to intercept and record communications on the network. Using this information, he obtained access to a second company's network, and deleted the company's entire database. For good measure, he left a message that said, "Hello, I have just hacked into your system. Have a nice day." The defendant's computer expertise in furtherance of these crimes earned him a special skills enhancement adding up to a twenty-seven-month prison term (US Department of Justice 2001b).

But the special skills enhancement does have its limits in the digital age. In one case, the defendant, who had no formal training in computing, bought Adobe Page Maker, an off-the-shelf software package. He learned how to use the program with the assistance of a high school friend over the course of a week and began scanning and duplicating US currency. The district court held that the defendant made use of special skills, but the appeals court found that the defendant's computer skills were not "particularly sophisticated" compared to those in Petersen, and thus found that the enhancement was unwarranted (*United States v. Godman* 223 F.3d 320 [6th Cir 2000]).

A closer call was made in a case arising from website counterfeiting. The defendant registered a domain name, www.honolulu-marathon.com, which was very close to the official site of the Honolulu Marathon Association, www.honolulu-marathon.org. He then created a website almost identical to the official site, but which also contained an online registration form in Japanese to receive registrants' credit card numbers (no such facility was available on the official site). The defendant was convicted of wire fraud in the US District Court; the court found that he "was skilled at accessing and manipulating computer systems" and imposed the special skills enhancement. On appeal, the court held that the skills required to counterfeit a Web page were more like Godman's than Petersen's, and not in the class of "pilots, lawyers, doctors, accountants, chemists, and demolition experts." The special skills enhancement of this sentence was disallowed (*United States v. Lee* 296 F. 3d 792 [9th Cir 2002]).

As digital technology becomes increasingly pervasive in everyday life, it thus appears that only those truly expert in computing will receive sentence enhancements for the application of their talents in furtherance of crime. Ordinary offenders will receive ordinary sentences.

RESTRICTIONS ACCOMPANYING SUPERVISED PROBATION AND FOLLOWING RELEASE FROM CUSTODY

Another consideration in sentencing cybercriminals concerns what restrictions, if any, should be placed on the offender as conditions of probation or parole. It is quite common, for example, to require that an offender refrain from consuming alcohol or drugs; convicted child sex offenders are often prohibited from associating with children. Computer criminals may be required to forfeit the equipment used in the commission of an offence; this is appropriate as long as the equipment in question is theirs, and not their employer's or someone else's. Somewhat more controversial are restrictions on the offender's access to, and use of, digital technology.

Perhaps the most prominent case to date is that of Kevin Mitnick, who was subject to a complete prohibition (without prior approval of his probation officer) on the possession or use of practically any kind of equipment that could be used to access a computer system or network. He was further prevented from serving as a consultant or advisor to anyone engaged in computer-related activity. Mitnick appealed against this order on the grounds that it was overly excessive and infringed on his First Amendment rights. The Appeals Court, however, held that the conditions were reasonable in light of the appellant's record of recidivism.

POST-RELEASE RESTRICTIONS IMPOSED ON KEVIN MITNICK

Without the prior express written approval of the probation officer, the defendant shall not possess or use, for any purpose, the following:

- Any computer hardware equipment
- Any computer software programs
- Modems
- Any computer-related peripheral or support equipment
- Portable laptop computers, "personal information assistants," and derivatives
- Cellular telephones
- Televisions or other instruments of communication equipped with online, Internet, World Wide Web, or other computer network access
- Any other electronic equipment, presently available or new technology that becomes available, that can be converted to or has as its function the ability to act as a

(*continued*)

computer system or to access a computer system, computer network, or telecommunications network (except defendant may possess a "land line" telephone)

- The defendant shall not be employed in or perform services for any entity engaged in the computer, computer software, or telecommunications business and shall not be in any capacity wherein he has access to computers or computer-related equipment or software

- The defendant shall not access computers, computer networks, or other forms of wireless communications himself or through third parties

- The defendant shall not act as a consultant or advisor to individuals or groups engaged in any computer-related activity

- The defendant shall not acquire or possess any computer codes (including computer passwords), cellular phone access codes, or other access devices that enable the defendant to use, acquire, exchange, or alter information in a computer or telecommunications database system

- The defendant shall not use or possess any data encryption device, program, or technique for computers

- The defendant shall not alter or possess any altered telephone, telephone equipment, or any other communications-related equipment

- The defendant shall only use his true name and not use any alias or other false identity. (Painter 2001, 44-5)

The ubiquity of digital technology may make restrictions as severe as those imposed on Mitnick a thing of the past. In a more recent case, the offender was prohibited from possessing or using a computer equipped with a modem allowing access to any part of the Internet. He appealed successfully, the judge observing that "such a ban renders modern life—in which, for example, the government strongly encourages taxpayers to file their returns electronically, more and more commerce is conducted online, and where vast amounts of government information are communicated via website—exceptionally difficult" (*United States v. Holm* 326 F 3d 872 C.A. 7 [2003]).

It therefore appears that restrictions imposed on cybercriminals will be less stringent. A more recent judgment indicates the kinds of strategies likely to be adopted in the future: "[M]ore narrowly-tailored restriction on Mr. Crume's computer use through a prohibition on accessing certain categories of websites and Internet content and can sufficiently ensure his compliance with this condition through some combination of random searches and software that filters objectionable material" (*United States v. Crume, 422 F.3d 728 [8th Cir. 2005]* at 733).

[8]

CONCLUSION: THE FUTURE OF CYBERCRIME AND ITS CONTROL

Society will continue to benefit from all the advantages bestowed upon us by digital technology. New applications, as yet unforeseen, will revolutionize the way we do things. But these developments will also provide new opportunities for criminals. Cybercrime will continue to challenge us. As more and more people from the less advantaged side of the digital divide cross over and enjoy more of the benefits of digital technology, they will contribute to the ranks of potential offenders and prospective victims. The arms race between those who seek to refine criminal applications of high technology and those who would interdict them will continue.

The challenges presented by the increasing sophistication of cybercrime require both individuals and organizations to be aware of the risks that they face. They must also maintain the capacity to prevent attacks whenever possible and to respond to those attacks that do occur. Cybercrime is sufficiently diverse and widespread that its effective prevention and control will require the efforts of many individuals and institutions. Just as police in Western industrial societies acknowledge that the effective reduction of terrestrial crime will require partnerships with industry and with the community, so it is with responses to cybercrime. Let us explore the most productive strategies to combat cybercrime from the perspective of routine activity theory. We will then revisit the role of private actors in law enforcement, including those actors to whom one might refer to as "cyber vigilantes." Following a discussion of legislative issues, we conclude with some observations on the future of cybercrime.

MOTIVATION

Prospects for reducing the supply of motivated offenders must be regarded as limited. As noted earlier, the motivations for many types of cybercrime are deeply engrained in the human behavioral repertoire. There is not a great deal that can be done to make people less greedy, less lustful, and less vengeful, in cyberspace or on the ground. Moreover, the idea of "pulling the plug" and restricting access to digital technology is becoming increasingly unrealistic, even for convicted offenders as a condition of their parole. Digital technology is now ubiquitous.

This is not to say that constructive work can be done at the margins to improve civility in cyberspace. Regardless of when people become introduced to digital technology, they are in a position to learn basic rules of etiquette. A culture of cyber civility can be learned. If informal socialization processes are insufficient to impress upon people what kinds of behaviors are unacceptable, governments appear more than willing to step in. Among the functions of the criminal law is the reaffirmation of society's values, and (at least in the United States) the stiff penalties prescribed for acts such as denial of service, disseminating child pornography, or software piracy make at least some would-be offenders think twice.

There was a time in America when overt expressions of racism were socially acceptable. Now they are not. At the dawn of the digital age, the hacker's ethic and the view that all information should be free were widely embraced and were not forcefully challenged (Levy 1984, p. 27). They are now.

One imaginative suggestion for changing hacker culture is to sponsor hack-in contests, offering positive incentives for those who might seek to channel their energies in lawful ways. The prospect of legitimate employment in the information security industry may be attractive to some hackers (Wible 2003). The closest terrestrial equivalents would appear to be the urban art movement that seeks to transform graffitists into muralists, and programs to provide training in automobile repair to young people implicated in motor vehicle theft. Such a program might divert a few individuals from engaging in illegal hacking, but its potential effects on the determinedly rebellious or the hacker for hire are certainly questionable. Nor would strategies like this be generalizable to child pornographers or fraudsters. We noted earlier how technology, by enhancing social distance between offender and prospective victim, can reduce inhibition on the part of the former.

OPPORTUNITY

The first line of defense against cybercrime is self-defense. Individuals and institutions with assets to protect are well advised to take basic security precautions commensurate with the risks they face. Individual users, for example, are urged to safeguard their passwords and PIN numbers and should invest in basic security software such as virus scanners. Organizations such as financial institutions, major retailers, and government agencies that may be attractive targets are likely to invest more heavily in IT security.

Market forces too will militate in favor of cybercrime control. While initial system architecture and software applications were designed for convenience (often at the expense of security), today security is given a higher priority. Since system integrity depends almost entirely on software, products are being designed for greater robustness, with fewer accessible "back doors."

Security and prosperity in cyberspace will depend significantly on market forces. Those financial institutions that provide secure platforms for online banking will flourish; those who do not will wither. Those companies that develop operating systems that optimize user friendliness and security will earn billions. The software and entertainment industries are devoting considerable energies to the development of technologies that will make their products more difficult for information pirates to reproduce.

New technologies of access control such as biometric authentication have tremendous potential to contribute to the "hardening" of electronic targets. As the cost of these technologies decreases, and as their accuracy improves, this will significantly reduce opportunities for unauthorized access to information systems. For the time being, however, the state of information security resembles where automobile safety was seventy years ago. The advent of seat belts, air bags, and the development of

BIOMETRIC AUTHENTICATION

The United Kingdom Biometrics Working Group (2006) defines biometric authentication as "the automated means of recognising a living person through the measurement of distinguishing physiological or behavioural traits." Biometric techniques include the following:

Signature dynamics: Differences in pressure and writing speed at specific points in the signature

Typing patterns: Time intervals between characters and overall speeds and patterns

Fingerprint scanners: Unique features of fingerprints

Hand or palm geometry: Lengths and angles of individual fingers

Facial recognition: Location of the nose and eyes, configuration of eye sockets, areas around cheekbones, and the sides of the mouth

Voice recognition: Verification of speech patterns

Eye scans: Distinguishing characteristics of retina or iris

(Kay 2005)

technologies to help automobiles and their passengers withstand crashes have significantly reduced the risks of road travel. One hopes that greater attention will be paid by software developers to minimizing vulnerabilities in the years ahead. If this does not occur, we will continue to be plagued by crashes of a different nature (Blunden 2014).

GUARDIANSHIP

One of the most important strategies for the prevention and control of cybercrime is to increase public awareness of the risks that private individuals and institutions face, and how best to minimize them. This is important, given the finite capacity of the state to control what goes on in cyberspace. There may have been times and places when commerce and critical infrastructure were state monopolies, but this is certainly not the case today.

It might be said that guardianship begins at home. Few parents are perfect, and protection of children from electronic harm will sooner or later clash with a young person's desire for privacy and personal space. Some very creative work has been done by nongovernmental organizations to confront the risks posed by information technology. Netsafe, an Internet Safety Group in New Zealand that has received international recognition, is one such example.[1] Netsafe provides basic information for parents, schools, small businesses, and other organizations on how to maintain basic computer security.

A significant component of capable guardianship is the prospective offender's perception that he or she is under surveillance. To continue the analogy with motor vehicle safety, red-light and speed cameras provide guardianship, as does the random testing of motorists for blood alcohol content.

To be sure, there are certain steps that individuals can take to mask their identity, cover their tracks, or conceal the content of their communications. Those of us who engage in Internet banking are grateful that our account numbers and access codes are shielded from public view. We are usually grateful that banks place a limit on the number and amount of withdrawals that we are allowed to make in a given period. On more than one occasion, I have been slightly embarrassed, but essentially pleased, to be contacted by my bank and queried about unusual charges made with my credit card. The bank was reassured to learn that the charges were all made by me.

PLURALISTIC PREVENTION AND CONTROL OF CYBERCRIME

Few if any governments in the world today are able to single-handedly provide for the security and prosperity of their citizens. This is no less the case in cyberspace than on the ground. Governments depend on the cooperation of various institutions in civil society. It follows that securing cyberspace will also necessarily be a pluralistic endeavor. This will entail a combination of technology, relevant crime prevention strategies, and up-to-date laws. Predictive technical measures for understanding common malware behaviors will remain a key focus (Alazab and Ventrakaman 2013).

Manufacturers, whether motivated by a spirit of good corporate citizenship, consumer demand, or by the specter of products liability litigation, have begun to design software and hardware products that are less vulnerable to criminal exploitation. Entire industries have developed to deliver security solutions, from encryption to firewalls, to biometric authentication devices. In November 2003, Microsoft announced the launch of its Antivirus Reward Program for information leading to the arrest and conviction of writers of malicious code. In 2013, Microsoft formed a public-private partnership with the FBI and financial services companies, which entailed criminal enforcement, seizure, and private civil action against one of the largest botnets then operating (Lerner 2014).

The Anti-Phishing Working Group (APWG) is a coalition of more than 2,000 organizations from the public, private, and nonprofit sectors that provides consumer advice, technical support, and a facility for reporting phishing overtures. Joint investigations involving public and private institutions are becoming increasingly common. One investigation involving cooperation between German law enforcement agencies, the US Secret Service and FBI, and Microsoft led to the arrest of an individual responsible for the Netsky and Sasser worms in May 2004.

In the United States, the Direct Marketing Association hired fifteen investigators to work with the FBI and other government agencies on antispam activity. The Australian High Tech Crime Centre in Canberra includes technicians from Australia's major financial institutions, whose salaries are paid by their banks and who work shoulder to shoulder with law enforcement officers.

Among those with a significant interest in controlling spam are Internet service providers, whose systems, figuratively speaking, groan under the weight of excessive e-mail. It was estimated in 2004, for example, that Microsoft's Hotmail service received two billion pieces of junk e-mail each day (Hansell 2004).

PRIVATE ENFORCEMENT

Corporate image is inherently valuable. When damaged, it can be very costly to repair. So it is that some companies engage private investigators to patrol cyberspace to ensure that their corporate websites have not been maliciously altered or counterfeit. Internet auction companies guard against use of their services to sell stolen goods or other contraband (Rustad 2001). The motion picture, music, and software industries have developed considerable capacity to detect piracy, to assist governments in investigation and prosecution, and to undertake private civil action against offenders (Tusikov 2015).

Private civil remedies may also contribute to the control of cybercrime. Just as street offences such as drug dealing can be addressed by private civil remedies such as nuisance laws (Mazerolle and Ransley 2006), so too can a variety of cybercrimes. Moreover, civil remedies require a significantly lower burden of proof— in common law countries, the balance of probability rather than reasonable doubt.

Numerous examples of the state creating specified rights, conferring them upon private parties, and leaving it up to those private parties to enforce, may be seen in the area of music and video piracy. There, the capacity and the priorities of public police may preclude criminal investigation of music, video, or software piracy, and a victim of piracy may be able to seek civil remedies. In the United States, the Recording Industry Association of America (RIAA) has sued over 10,000 individuals for allegedly pirating music online (Weber 2005). In 2003, the Motion Picture Association (MPA) achieved resolution of two civil actions in relation to DVD piracy in the Beijing Second Intermediate People's Court, and six cases in the People's Courts of Shanghai. The terms of the settlements included ceasing further replication and destroying all copies; making formal apologies; the payment of penalties averaging $10,000 per case; and an agreement to pay increased penalties if unauthorized replication recurs (MPA 2003a, 2003b).

Engineering institutions have emerged and evolved in furtherance of cybercrime control. In the aftermath of the Morris worm in 1988, a Computer Emergency Response Team (CERT) was established at Carnegie Mellon University in Pittsburgh to coordinate responses to Internet security problems (Carnegie-Mellon Software Engineering Institute 2005). CERT Members are alerted to potential security threats against their systems and advice on how best to avoid, minimize, and recover from damage (Carnegie-Mellon Software Engineering Institute, 2005). In 2003, A National Computer Emergency Readiness team (US-CERT) was established as part of the Department of Homeland Security.[2] Worldwide, there are more than 250 organizations with the acronym CERT who concern themselves with cybersecurity. It would appear that "coordinating the coordinators" will be a major challenge of the twenty-first century. This has begun to occur at international and regional levels under the auspices of FIRST, the global Forum of Incident Response and Security Teams.

Negligent management of one's computer systems can lead to significant problems. Failure to supervise adequately an employee's use of the office computer system can lead to difficulties if, in the course of unauthorized surfing or e-mailing, the system contracts a virus or is penetrated by a Trojan Horse. Harassment by one employee of another employee can land their employer in court. Because misuse of an organization's computer systems occurs from within their own ranks as well as at the hands of outsiders, a degree of inside guardianship is essential.

Depending on the jurisdiction, victims of cyber harassment or cyber bullying outside of the workplace may have a cause of action for invasion of privacy, emotional distress, or defamation. But even when such civil remedies may be available, they are by no means a panacea. Some victims may not be able to afford the legal expenses that a civil suit can entail. Moreover, victims may fear further harassment, intimidation, or retaliation if their identities are disclosed in the course of litigation (Citron 2014).

CYBER VIGILANTES

The appropriate role of private citizens in the control of cybercrime is a vexing issue. In cyberspace, as in the terrestrial world, it is usually not a good thing for a person to take the law into one's own hands. The reasons for this should be self-evident. Consistency and fairness in the application of law are arguably best done by the state.

The role of the private citizen in intelligence collection or law enforcement is not without precedent. Privateers and bounty hunters have a long, if not always glorious tradition in the United States. The lynch mobs of the late nineteenth and early twentieth centuries were a particularly dark chapter in American history. Indeed, one of the virtues of the modern state (in theory at least) has been the development of exacting procedures for the administration of criminal justice, within clearly defined structures of accountability.

Private citizens, even well-meaning ones, may not fully understand the consequences of their actions. For one, a hunt for pedophiles or terrorists in cyberspace may entail unauthorized access to, or interference with, a computer system, both of which are criminal offences. For another, a private sleuth may inadvertently interrupt an ongoing investigation or may contaminate a crime scene. A "counter-hacker," striking back at the apparent source of an intrusion, may be unaware that his or her target, the proximate source of the offending communication, may be a mere tool commandeered by the true offender. It is not difficult to inflict a great deal of damage in cyberspace, quite by accident.

The activities of private citizens vary in terms of intrusiveness. At one extreme are those who many encounter indicia of illegality in cyberspace, and basically ignore it. Next there are those who might call the matter to the attention of another private actor—perhaps a "cyber watchdog" or Internet safety group such as the Cyber Angels.[3] Others may see fit to report it to an appropriate authority such as the Securities and Exchange Commission,[4] the Internet Crime Complaint Center,[5] or the CyberTipline of the National Center for Missing & Exploited Children.[6] Online vigilante activity is quite common in China, where antisocial behavior and apparent corruption have been targeted by "netizens" with a view toward identifying the alleged offender and encouraging shaming or even civil or criminal penalties. The literal Chinese term for such activity is "human flesh search engine," but a more accurate translation would read "crowd-sourced investigation" (Gough 2013; Jacobs 2013; Chang and Leung 2015).

Some citizens patrol the public areas of cyberspace, looking for indicia of illegality. Alternatively, they can encounter crime by happenstance, in the course of "surfing the Web" or in an Internet chat room. Huey et al. (2013) report that some individuals engage in informal surveillance, seeking to identify whether persons registered as sex offenders have a presence in social networking communities such as Facebook and MySpace. Thompson (2009, p. 559) notes that volunteer groups monitor botnets and maintain blacklists of spam (see www.spamhaus.org/). Others "patrol" eBay auctions in search of apparent fraud. In some cases they have warned buyers or made exceptionally high bids in order to disrupt the auction (Schwartz 2004).

Some will go further, such as entering a chat room pretending to be a fourteen-year-old, arranging for a meeting in physical space, then showing up armed with a video camera.

Images may then be posted or the Web, or details may be referred to the police.[7]

Private citizens have been active in pursuing the perpetrators of advance-fee fraud schemes as well as child pornographers. Creating their own false identities, these "counter scammers" seek to engage the real fraudsters. The most benign simply lead the fraudster on, by engaging them in endless correspondence, or by such means as (falsely) assuring them that a payment is available for collection at a Western Union office in a distant city. Some seek to collect financial and technical information to refer to law enforcement agencies. Others seek to embarrass or humiliate the fraudster, by getting them to pose for photographs. At the extreme, some seek to disable fraudulent bank websites or break into the fraudsters' e-mail accounts to identify and warn prospective victims (Schiesel 2004). For many, it is a kind of sport.[8]

An interesting issue, by no means close to definitive resolution, relates to the extent to which the government should compel third parties to assist in the prevention and control of cybercrime. For example, service providers may be required to preserve records or other evidence in their possession when requested by the government, pending the issuance of a court order.[9] Some jurisdictions require data retention as a matter of routine. A number of jurisdictions in the United States and elsewhere require computer repair technicians or other IT professionals who encounter evidence of child pornography to report this to law enforcement (Brenner 2011).

In some cases, individuals or organizations may be tempted to take the law into their own hands. Majuca and Kesan (2009) report a number of retaliatory cyberattacks by various companies and by the US Department of Defense in response to electronic intrusions (see also Smith 2005). The principal of an Indian software firm claimed that his company had been engaged by the motion picture industry in response to piracy. The firm searched the Internet to find films that have been illegally uploaded and then sent the hosting server a request to remove the pirated content. Noncompliance with a second request was met with a denial of service attack. The firm has also claimed to have remotely destroyed pirated products in order to prevent further illegal use (Grubb 2010).

In the United States, the Bill of Rights protects a citizen against an illegal search by the government, but not by a private citizen. In general, evidence obtained as the result of an illegal search by government agents will be inadmissible in court. Evidence obtained illegally by a private actor will be admissible in criminal proceedings as long as the government did not encourage, or have prior knowledge of, the illegal action. The following anecdote raises interesting questions about private third-party involvement in cyber law enforcement:

In July 2000, a police officer in Montgomery, Alabama, received an e-mail message and an attached image from "unknownuser1069@hotmail .com." The message read:

> I found a child molester on the net. I'm not sure if he is abusing his own child or a child he kidnapped. He is from Montgomery, Alabama. As you see he is torturing the kid. She is 5-6 y.o. His face is seen clearly on some of the pictures. I know his name, Internet account, home address and I can see when he is online. What should I do? Can I send all the pics and info I have to these emails?
>
> Regards
>
> P.S. He is a doctor or a paramedic.

At the request of the police officer, "Unknownuser," who later revealed that he was from Istanbul, Turkey, provided the IP address, name, street address, and fax number of a local Montgomery doctor. Based on this information, police obtained the appropriate warrants and arrested the suspect, who was tried, convicted, and sentenced to seventeen and a half years of imprisonment.

Unknownuser was reluctant to identify himself to the police for one obvious reason. His access to the doctor's computer was obtained by illegal means. Unknownuser had posted a file containing a version of the subseven Trojan Horse virus to the news group "alt.binaries.pictures.erotica. pre-teen." He claimed to have identified 2,000 other collectors of child pornography in that manner.

The doctor's appeal was unsuccessful, the Court holding inter alia that Unknownuser's crime was not committed with the knowledge or encouragement of the government, and that the evidence obtained as a result was admissible (*United States v. Steiger* 318 F.3d 1039 C.A. 11 [Ala.] 2003).

But what about circumstances, such as those anticipated by mandatory reporting legislation, where computer repair technicians are required to report apparent child pornography to police? Could it not be said that such legislation not only encourages but also requires notification? The action required by the South Carolina Code is notification, not search (*United States v. Peterson* 294 F Supp. 2d 797 [D.S.C. November 25, 2003]). One might also note that a person would have a lesser expectation of privacy in handing his computer over to a repair facility than in using it in the security of his home, an important distinction under US law.

LEGISLATION

Governments will continue to play a major role in securing cyberspace. Governmental responses to cybercrime require first an adequate set of laws. Adequate substantive criminal legislation should be in place to prohibit current and emerging manifestations of cybercrime, and laws of evidence and procedure should facilitate investigation and prosecution, without encroaching upon human rights.

There are a number of issues that governments must consider in developing a legislative framework for the prevention and control of cybercrime. First is the substantive criminal law. It is important to spell out exactly which kind of conduct is criminal, and which is not. The rule of law requires the avoidance of vagueness and ambiguity. The ordinary citizen should know what behavior is permitted and what is forbidden. In those countries that adhere most closely to the rule of law, uncertainties in criminal statutes are to be resolved in favor of the defendant.

In some jurisdictions, the existing substantive criminal law will be adequate to embrace cybercrime. The elasticity of criminal legislation may be sufficient to cover many crimes, certainly the old crimes committed with new technologies. In other places, new legislation may be required. At the time the "I Love You" virus was released, there was no law in the Philippines that prohibited such activity. Two months later, the Philippine Congress enacted legislation to close this loophole.

A statute that criminalizes fraud, but only when perpetrated against human actors, may be challenged on the grounds that it does not extend to the deception of machinery. This would make it necessary to criminalize explicitly ATM-related fraud (*Kennison v. Daire* 160 CLR 129 [1986]). Certainly, a preference for technology-neutral language would be in order, given the risk that the law could become obsolete as a result of technological developments.

In many jurisdictions, laws relating to theft of or damage to property had to be revised in order to cover *intangible* property, such as software and entertainment products consisting of "zeroes and ones." Some new forms of harmful activity, such as unauthorized access to a computer or interfering with the lawful use of a computer, required new legislative prohibitions. The criminal procedure law—the law that governs the search for and seizure of evidence—must also be adapted to cyberspace. Techniques of investigation that were once the stuff of science fiction are now in common use. It is important that their use, and those who use them, be accountable and subject to the rule of law.

As the history of cybercrime litigation shows, governments cannot always be confident that existing laws are adequate to withstand the challenges of resourceful defense counsel. Legislators may therefore be tempted to insure themselves by enacting a "bulletproof" statute. Even when new laws may not be absolutely necessary, governments may enact redundant legislation for symbolic purposes, as a way of formally denouncing the crime in question.

HARMONIZATION OF CYBERCRIME LAWS

The borderless nature of cyberspace makes it important that laws of different countries around the world are as similar as possible. In the absence of comparable or common legislation, cybercriminals may seek out cybercriminal "havens" from which they can operate with impunity.

There are a number of different areas in which a degree of international consistency is desirable. These include the substantive criminal law, laws relating to searches of computers, networks, and systems; the collection and preservation of electronic evidence; and international cooperation. One might also add the legal liabilities of internet service providers for the prevention and control of cybercrime (UNODC 2013).

Nations on the privileged side of the digital divide tend to have adequate legislation in place. The most widely embraced model is the Council of Europe Cybercrime Convention, to date the most widespread and comprehensive initiative in international cooperation in cybercrime control. The convention seeks to achieve a degree of consistency in substantive criminal law, evidence, and procedure, as well as expedited mutual assistance in cases of cybercrime committed across national frontiers. Even during its long drafting stage (over four years and producing twenty-seven drafts), it provided guidance for non-European states involved in developing their own legislation. The Council of Europe formally adopted the Convention on Cybercrime in Budapest in November 2000, and it came into force in July 2004.[10] Although the Convention has been embraced by countries as diverse as Canada, Japan, the United States, and South Africa, it has not been universally welcomed. Some states still harbor unpleasant memories of their experience at the hands of European colonial exploitation and are disinclined to embrace the Convention because of its provenance. Others have expressed reluctance to sign the treaty because they were not involved in the drafting process and thereby feel a lack of ownership. Russia, in particular, is very sensitive about issues of sovereignty and takes strong objections to those provisions of the Convention that provide for remote, cross-border searches.

There are other regional or international instruments, including those established under the League of Arab States, African intergovernmental organizations, and the Commonwealth of Independent States (the former Soviet Republics). In addition, there are various model laws available to those nations lacking adequate legislative coverage of cybercrime and its investigation. However, because of the lack of truly global arrangements, a number of commentators have called for a new convention to be developed under UN auspices (UNODC 2013).

Legislative initiatives to control spam have been introduced in a number of countries; in the United States, the CAN SPAM Act became law in 2003. Among the more popular features are the requirements that the e-mail in question:

- Contain clear and conspicuous identification as an advertisement
- Include "opt out" instructions permitting the recipient to exclude future unsolicited communications from the same source
- Include an "unsubscribe" facility

Legislation may also make it an offence to use a false or misleading header or deceptive subject line. Some jurisdictions have introduced prohibitions on the use of electronic address-harvesting tools and of harvested address lists, predicates to the dissemination of Spam. In addition to the criminal sanction, it may be possible to use other remedies. Civil law may allow suits for trespass to chattel; purveyors of spam may be liable for interfering with the lawful use of computer systems if a system's disks are damaged or if an individual's lawful use is impeded by spam (Sorkin 2001; Magee 2003). Microsoft and a number of other prominent Internet service providers have used the civil justice system against spammers.

There may be no perfect solution for the problem of spam. Purveyors of "V1agra" can defeat blocking and filtering technologies. Some of these technologies can be too restrictive, screening out communications that one might actually want to see. It is difficult for legislative drafters to differentiate spam from other commercial communications, or indeed from political communications, which are usually subject to a degree of protection in democratic societies. The risk of overregulation, with the adverse unintended consequences that so often accompany legislative intervention, cannot be overlooked. And, as more and more commerce occurs in the online environment, it is important not to discourage legitimate commercial activity. A recent survey by the UN Office of Drugs and Crime reported fewer than one third of reporting countries had made sending spam a criminal offense (UNODC 2013).

INTERNATIONAL COOPERATION

International cooperation in the prevention and control of cybercrime has intensified with the global increase in connectivity. Understandably, initiatives began in the industrialized world, where the risks of cybercrime were most apparent. In December 1997, the eight major industrialized nations (the G8) drew up a ten-point plan to confront transnational cybercrime. The major pillars were the development of a solid legislative base and the development of capacity among criminal justice professionals to deal with these crimes.

As noted earlier, the Council of Europe Convention on Cybercrime seeks to achieve a degree of consistency in substantive criminal law, evidence, and procedure, as well as expedited mutual assistance in cases of cybercrime committed across national frontiers.

Despite the progress made to date, insufficiencies abound in the capacities of many states to defend against cybercrime. The 2013 report by the UN Office of Drugs and Crime suggests that poorer countries, despite the growing penetration of digital technology, still lack adequate legislation and the means to enforce it. Not only does this have the potential to retard economic development (given the infrastructure for economic growth that digital technology provides), it also invites the exploitation of poor countries as criminal havens by determined offenders.

THE FUTURE OF CYBERCRIME

Cybercrime is a moveable feast. It is tempting, but risky, to try to anticipate what the future holds in store for us. In 1990, I was asked by the Australian Government to estimate the kinds of problems that they would be likely to encounter in the year 2000. I suggested that "junk faxes" might become a problem. The problems of spam or denial of service attacks were nowhere on my radar screen. What we can say with certainty is that every new technology or device will have criminal applications.

Consider, for example, "cloud computing," mentioned earlier. Despite the economies that it brings to the task, cloud computing is not without its vulnerabilities. The same technologies and applications are no less valuable to illicit exploitation than they are to legitimate use (Mills 2012). Garfinkel (2011) reports that facilities such as Amazon's Elastic Computing Cloud (EC2) permit access to formidable computing power, and, as a result, an encryption password that once would have required years to break can now be obtained in a matter of days.

Sharing of data and applications may be appropriate in large-scale collaborative undertakings. Where data security is critical, however, data held in multi-tenancy arrangements may be vulnerable to inadvertent disclosure or intentional unauthorized access. Collective storage of data creates a large target and, in theory at least, more points of entry and, by definition, windows of vulnerability. Clouds are also used to host illicit content such as malware, pirated software and entertainment, and child pornography. As ostensibly legitimate hosting services, they may be accorded a degree of trust (Vijayan 2013).

We may be confident of one thing: Technology will not stand still. For many people around the world, new technologies and applications, unforeseeable today, will be introduced in our lifetime. These technologies will expand our capacities and make life more exciting and fulfilling. Alas, they will also provide new opportunities for criminals. In the words of Rosoff, Pontell, and Tillman's (1998) "First Law of Electronic Crime," *If it can be done, someone will do it.*

THE INTERNET OF THINGS

One window into the future may reveal development in what has been referred to as "the Internet of things." By this is meant the interconnection of most, if not all objects, through the Internet. This has been referred to as "web 3.0," "semantic web," "ubiquitous computing," and "pervasive computing"—the terms are interchangeable. A glimpse of this emerging trend may be seen in those findings from the 2014 Eurobarometer survey (European Commission 2015), which reported a sharp increase over the previous year in the use of smartphones and touchscreen tablets to access the Internet. By the end of 2014, over 60 percent of European internet users had used smartphones for Internet access. The connectivity of smartphones appears destined to increase substantially, and the UNODC (2013) estimates that by the year 2020, the number of networked devices in the world will outnumber people by 6 to 1.

A very simplistic example of such connectivity can be seen in the relationship of a supermarket checkout scanner to the system of inventory control. Real-time monitoring of the sales of a particular product will inform systems for just-in-time delivery of replacement stock. Another application is predictive search, based on holistic scanning of one's e-mails, appointment calendar, social network and other digital activity, and geo-location data. This can then serve as the basis for automatic notifications to one's cell phone; imagine being advised automatically when it is time to leave for a dinner reservation, based on one's location, mode of transport, and real-time traffic conditions. Such applications as these are now with us, and in many respects, make our lives easier, safer, better informed, and generally more pleasant.

The bad news is that these technologies are available to criminals no less than to us honest folk. And you can bet that this is not lost on imaginative criminal minds. Presentations to recent Black Hat and Defcon conferences suggest some possible exploits (Bilton 2013). The remote immobilization of automobiles on the highway, deactivation of home (or commercial, or government) security systems, and the disabling of medical devices are but three generic examples. Perlroth (2013) reports that a commonly used system supporting digital hotel room keys contained flaws that can easily be exploited by a determined hacker. Pranksters would no doubt be attracted to the idea of toilets that can be made to overflow and to digital refrigerators that can be turned off.

Internet-connected camera systems, even baby monitors, and "smart TVs" have already fallen victims to hackers (Wood 2015). Technologies of 3D printing permit the production of actual firearms. The code for a weapon can be transmitted online, and the instrument produced in a physical location on the other side of the world, bypassing customs and postal inspectors (Goodman 2015).

Dupont (2013) and Goodman (2015) have discussed a number of new and emerging technologies that may be vulnerable to criminal exploitation. Other commentators have shown or suggested how a number of systems based on digital technology may be compromised remotely, with serious consequences. The remote commandeering of unmanned aerial vehicles and other robotic devices also seems likely. In December 2012, Iran claimed to have captured a US surveillance drone, after having compromised its control systems (Erdbrink 2012). Bilton (2013) reports that it is now possible to connect two human brains over the Internet (see also Rao 2013a, 2013b; Wolpaw and Wolpaw 2012). Rao (2013b) reported that in one case, scientists were able to control a person's hand movement by thinking about it. In another, they were able to influence movement of a rat's tail in a similar manner. It may be premature to speculate on the extent to which brain-to-brain technology or computer-to-brain technology may be vulnerable to criminal exploitation (by both traditional criminals and governments), but such technologies are no longer the stuff of science fiction.

A century ago, the famous philosopher Santayana observed that those who forget the past are condemned to repeat it. Today, those who ignore the future are in for a rude shock when it arrives.

ENDNOTES

CHAPTER 3

1. http://www.phrack.org/(accessed July 7, 2015); http://www.2600.com/ (accessed July 7, 2015).
2. http://www.justice.gov/criminal/cybercrime/press-releases/2004/sabathia Plea.htm (accessed July 7, 2015).
3. For a dramatic example of a digitally constructed hoax photograph, see http://en.wikipedia.org/wiki/Helicopter_Shark#mediaviewer/ File:Helicopter_Shark_Thumb.jpg (accessed July 7, 2015).
4. See http://www.2600.com/hacked_pages/old_archives.html (accessed July 7, 2015).
5. http://www.fas.org/irp/offdocs/ppd/ppd-20.pdf (accessed July 7, 2015)
6. http://www.usdoj.gov/criminal/cybercrime/juvenilepld.htm (accessed March 9, 2006; https://archive.is/ie3J4 (accessed July 7, 2015)
7. http://news.bbc.co.uk/2/hi/science/nature/1541252.stm (accessed August 17, 2015).
8. http://www.sclqld.org.au/caselaw/QCA/browse/2002/+100 (accessed July 2, 2015).
9. https://www.google.ca/search?q=ISIS+hostage+beheadings&lr=&source= lnms&tbm=vid&sa=X&ei=dNfrVLzUGaGzmwWI04GYAQ&ved=0C AgQ_AUoAQ&biw=960&bih=467&cad=cbv&sei=qNfrVPyoHeW9mgW Uh4DgDQ (accessed 7 July 2015)
10. https://www.caselaw.nsw.gov.au/decision/54a63a733004de94513dabe8 (accessed July 2, 2015)
11. http://www.austlii.edu.au/au/cases/vic/VSC/2007/425.html (accessed July 2, 2015).

CHAPTER 5

1. https://www.bankofamerica.com/privacy/external-resources.go (accessed July 7, 2015).
2. BBC News 2001 Mafiaboy hacker jailed 13 September. http://news.bbc .co.uk/1/hi/sci/tech/1541252.stm (accessed July 7, 2015).

3. (CyberSource 2004) 5th Annual Online Fraud Report: Credit Card Fraud Trends and Merchants' Response. http://www.security.iia.net.au/downloads/2004_fraud_report.pdf (visited March 9, 2006); (Cyber Source 2015) Online Fraud Management Benchmarks http://www.cybersource.com/resources/collateral/Resource_Center/whitepapers_and_reports/CYBS-Fraud-Benchmark-Report.pdf?utm_campaign=2015%20Fraud%20Report%20Form%20Auto%20Responder&utm_medium=email&utm_source=Eloqua (accessed July 7, 2015).

CHAPTER 6

1. http://www.cpha.ca/en/conferences/fraud.aspx (accessed July 7, 2015); http://www.uia.org/fraud-monitor (accessed July 7, 2015); http://www.scamorama.com/conferences.html (accessed July 7, 2015).
2. https://www.torproject.org/press/press.html.en (accessed July 7, 2015).

CHAPTER 7

1. *Regulation of Investigatory Powers Act* (2000) ss 49-55; *Crimes Act 1914 (Cth)*, s. 3LA.
2. *R v. Steven George Hourmouzis*, County Court, Melbourne (Stott J) 30 October 2000 http://www.countycourt.vic.gov.au/CA256D90000479B3/Lookup/Judgments_H/$file/hourmouz.pdf (accessed December 29, 2005); http://asic.gov.au/about-asic/media-centre/find-a-media-release/2001-releases/01166-two-years-jail-suspended-for-internet-spammer/ (accessed July 7, 2015).
3. http://www.netaddiction.com (accessed July 7, 2015).
4. United States v. O'Keefe 461 F.3d 1338 (11th Cir. 2006).

CHAPTER 8

1. http://www.netsafe.org.nz (accessed July 7, 2015).
2. http://www.us-cert.gov (accessed July 7, 2015).
3. http://www.cyberangels.org (accessed July 7, 2015).
4. enforcement@sec.gov
5. http://www.ic3.gov (accessed July 7, 2015).
6. http://www.missingkids.com/cybertipline/ (accessed July 7, 2015).
7. http://www.perverted-justice.com (accessed July 7, 2015).
8. http://www.scamorama.com (accessed July 7, 2015).
9. 18 U.S.C. s 2703 (f).
10. http://conventions.coe.int/Treaty/en/Treaties/Html/185.htm (accessed July 7, 2015).

REFERENCES

Ablon, Lillian, Libicki, Martin, and Golay, Andrea. (2014). *Markets for Cybercrime Tools and Stolen Data: Hackers' Bazaar.* Santa Monica, CA: RAND Corporation.

Afronline. (2010, 16 September). "Protest in Mozambique: The Power of SMS." http://www.afronline.org/?p=8680 (accessed 7 July, 2015).

Alazab, Mamoun and Broadhurst, Roderic (2014) "Spam and Criminal Activity" http://papers.ssrn.com/sol3/papers.cfm?abstract_id=2467423 (accessed July 2, 2015).

Alazab, Mamoun, and Venkatraman, Sitalakshmi. (2013). "Detecting Malicious Behaviour Using Supervised Learning Algorithms of the Function Calls." *International Journal of Electronic Security and Digital Forensics*, 5(2), 90–109. doi:10.1504/IJESDF.2013.055047

Alazab, Mamoun, Venkatraman, Sitalakshmi, Watters, Paul, Alazab, Moutaz, and Alazab, Ammar. (2012). "Cybercrime: The Case of Obfuscated Malware" *Global Security, Safety and Sustainability & e-Democracy*, 99, 204–211. doi: 10.1007/978-3-642-33448-1_28

Al Hayat Media. (2014). *Flames of War.* http://news.yahoo.com/video/islamic-state-release-propaganda-film-153137452.html (accessed July 7, 2014).

Allen, Jonathan, Forrest, Sarah, Levi, Michael, Hanna, Roy, Sutton, Michael, and Wilson, Debbie. (2005). *Fraud and Technology Crimes: Findings from the 2002/03 British Crime Survey and 2003 Offending, Crime and Justice Survey.* London, UK: Home Office http://webarchive.nationalarchives.gov.uk/20110220105210/rds.homeoffice.gov.uk/rds/pdfs05/rdsolr3405.pdf (accessed July 7, 2015).

Anderson, Ross, Barton, Chris, Bohme, Rainer, Clayton, Richard, van Eeten, Michel J.G., Levi, Michael, Moore, Tyler, and Savage, Stefan. (2012, 25–26 June). *Measuring the Cost of Cybercrime.* Paper presented to the 11th Annual Workshop on the Economics of Information Security, Berlin, http://weis2012.econinfosec.org/papers/Anderson_WEIS2012.pdf (accessed July 7, 2015).

Anti Phishing Working Group. (2014). *Phishing Activity Trends Report, 2nd Quarter 2014.* https://apwg.org/apwg-news-center/APWG-News/ (accessed July 7, 2015).

Ashcroft, John. (2004). *The Regpay Child Pornography Indictment.* http://www.usdoj.gov/opa/pr/2004/January/04_ag_021.htm (accessed July 7, 2015).

Ashmore, William C. (2009) *Impact of Alleged Russian Cyber Attacks*. School of Advanced Military Studies, United States Army Command and General Staff College, Fort Leavenworth, KA. http://www.dtic.mil/cgi-bin/GetTRDoc?AD= ADA504991 (accessed August 17, 2015).

Associated Press. (1999). *Man Guilty of Internet Stalking*. http://www.bayinsider.com/news/1999/01/20/stalking.html (accessed July 1, 1999).

Association of Chief Police Officers (UK) (2012) *ACPO Good Practice Guide for DigitalEvidence*.http://library.college.police.uk/docs/acpo/digital-evidence-2012.pdf(accessed July 8, 2015)

AusCERT. (2005). *2005 Australian Computer Crime and Security Survey*. http://www.auscert.org.au/images/ACCSS2005.pdf (accessed January 16, 2006).

AusCERT. (2015). *Incident Management Service*. https://www.auscert.org.au/services/incident-management-services (accessed July 7, 2015).

The Australian. (2014, 4 February). "Nigeria 'scammer' Orowo Jesse Omokoh Held over Death of Australian Jette Jacobs." *The Australian*. http://www.theaustralian.com.au/news/nation/nigeria-scammer-orowo-jesse-omokoh-held-over-death-of-australian-jette-jacobs/story-e6frg6nf-1226817168140 (accessed July 7, 2015).

Babchishin, Kelly M., Hanson, R. Karl, and Hermann, Chantal A. (2011). "The Characteristics of Online Sex Offenders: A Meta-Analysis." *Sexual Abuse: A Journal of Research and Treatment*, 23(1), 92–123.

Bailey, Eric (2001, 9 March) "3 Men Indicted in Alleged Scheme to Boost EBay Art Bids" *Los Angeles Times* http://articles.latimes.com/2001/mar/09/business/fi-35394 (accessed July 8, 2015).

Bamford, James. (2008). *The Shadow Factory: The NSA from 9/11 to the Eavesdropping on America*. New York, NY: Random House.

Barlow, John Perry. (1996). *A Declaration of the Independence of Cyberspace*. https://projects.eff.org/~barlow/Declaration-Final.html (accessed July 7, 2015).

BBC. (2013). *China Employs Two Million Microblog Monitors State Media Say*. http://www.bbc.com/news/world-asia-china-24396957 (accessed July 7, 2015).

Beh, Hazel Glenn. (2001). "Physical Losses in Cyberspace." *Connecticut Insurance Law Journal*, 8, 55–86.

Benzmiller, Heather. (2013). "The Cyber-Samaritans: Exploring Criminal Liability for the 'Innocent' Bystanders of Cyberbullying." *Northwestern University Law Review*, 107(2), 927–962.

Bernstein, Richard. (2006, 10 May). "Cannibal Gets Life Sentence in Retrial." *The New York Times*. http://query.nytimes.com/gst/fullpage.html?res=980 4EFDF173EF933A25756C0A9609C8B63 (accessed July 7, 2015).

Blunden, Bill, and Cheung, Violet. (2014). *Behold a Pale Farce: Cyberwar, Threat Inflation, & the Malware Industrial Complex*. Walterville, OR: TrineDay.

Bray, Chad. (2015, 18 February). "Swiss Prosecutors Search Offices of HSBC Unit."*TheNewYorkTimes*.http://dealbook.nytimes.com/2015/02/18/geneva-prosecutors-open-inquiry-into-hsbc-swiss-unit/?_r=0 (accessed July 7, 2015).

Brenner, Susan. (2011). "Defining Cybercrime: A Review of Federal and State Law." In *Cybercrime: The Investigation, Prosecution and Defense of a Computer-Related Crime* (3rd ed.), edited by R. D. Clifford, pp. 15–104. Raleigh, NC: Carolina Academic Press.

Brenner, Susan, Carrier, Brian, and Jenniger, Jef. (2004). "The Trojan Horse Defense in Cybercrime Cases." *Santa Clara Computer and High Tech Law Journal*, 21, 1–53.

Broadhurst, Roderic, Grabosky, Peter, Alazab, Mamoun, and Chon, Steve. (2014). "Organizations and Cyber Crime: An Analysis of the Nature of Groups Engaged in Cyber Crime." *International Journal of Cyber Criminology*, 8(1), 1–20.

Buchanan, Tom, and Whitty, Monica T. (2014) "The Online Dating Romance Scam: Causes and Consequences of Victimhood." *Psychology, Crime & Law*, 20(3), 261–283.

Burgess, Ann W., Carretta, Carrie M., and Burgess, Allen G. (2012). "Patterns of Federal Internet Offenders: A Pilot Study." *Journal of Forensic Nursing*, 8, 3, 112–121.

Business Software Alliance. (2013). *The Compliance Gap: BSA Global Software Survey*. http://globalstudy.bsa.org/2013/ (accessed July 7, 2015).

Carnegie-Mellon Software Engineering Institute. (2005). *Cert Coordination Centre*. http://www.cert.org/ (accessed July 7, 2015).

Casey, Eoghan. (2011). *Digital Evidence and Computer Crime: Forensic Science, Computers and the Internet* (3rd ed.). San Diego, CA: Academic Press.

CFCA. (2013). *PBX Hacking 2013 Global Fraud Loss Survey 2013*. http://www.cfca.org/press.php (accessed July 7, 2015).

Chan, Darrell, and Wang Dawei. (2015). "Profiling Cybercrime Perpetrators in China and Its Policy Countermeasures." In *Cybercrime Risks and Responses: Eastern and Western Perspectives*, edited by R. G. Smith, R. C-C. Cheung, and L. Y-C. Lau, pp. 206-222. Houndmills, UK: Palgrave Macmillan.

Chang, Lennon Yao-Chung. (2012). *Cybercrime in the Greater China Region*. Cheltenham, UK: Edward Elgar.

Chang, Lennon Yao-Chung, and Leung, Andy K. H. (2015). "An Introduction to Cyber-Crowdsourcing (Human Flesh Searching) in the Greater China Region." *Cybercrime Risks and Responses: Eastern and Western Perspectives*, edited by R. G. Smith, R. C-C. Cheung, and L. Y-C. Lau, pp. 240-252. Houndmills, UK: Palgrave Macmillan.

Chaudhuri, Sabiira. (2014, 18 February). "Cost of Replacing Credit Cards after Target Breach Estimated at $200 Million." *Wall Street Journal*. http://www.wsj.com/news/articles/SB10001424052702304675504579391080333769014 (accessed July 7, 2015).

Choe, Sang-Hun. (2014, 11 September). "Former South Korean Spy Chief Convicted in Online Campaign against Liberals." *The New York Times*. http://www.nytimes.com/2014/09/12/world/asia/former-south-korean-spy-chief-convicted-in-online-campaign-against-liberals.html?hp&action=click&pgtype=Homepage&

version=HpHeadline&module=second-column-region&region=top-news&WT.nav=top-news (accessed July 7, 2015).

Choo, K.K. Raymond, and Grabosky, Peter. (2013). "Cyber Crime." In *Oxford Handbook of Organized Crime*, edited by Paoli, pp. 482-499. Oxford, UK: Oxford University Press.

Citron, Danielle. (2014). *Hate Crimes in Cyberspace*. Cambridge, MA: Harvard Univrsity Press.

CNBC. (2014, 3 October). *JPMorgan Cyberattack Hits 76M households*. http://www.cnbc.com/id/102049505# (accessed July 7, 2015).

CNN. (2015). "Iran Hacked an American Casino, US Says." *CNN Money* http://money.cnn.com/2015/02/27/technology/security/iran-hack-casino/(accessed July 7, 2015).

Cohen, L., and Felson, M. (1979). "Social Change and Crime Rate Trends: A Routine Activity Approach." *American Sociological Review*, 44, 588–608.

Coleman, Gabriella. (2014). *Hacker, Hoaxer, Whistleblower, Spy: The Many Faces of Anonymous*. London, UK: Verso Books.

Cooper, Helene. (2015, 12 January). "ISIS Is Cited in Hacking of Central Command's Twitter and YouTube Accounts." *The New York Times*. http://www.nytimes.com/2015/01/13/us/isis-is-cited-in-hacking-of-central-commands-twitter-feed.html (accessed July 7 2015).

Cooper, Michael, Schmidt, Michael, and Schmitt, Eric (2013, 23 April) "Boston Suspects Are Seen as Self-Taught and Fueled by Web" *The New York Times*. http://www.nytimes.com/2013/04/24/us/boston-marathon-bombing-developments.html?pagewanted=all (accessed 7 July 2015).

Crimmins, Danielle, Falk, Courtney, Fowler, Susan, Gravel, Caitlin, Kourementis, Michael, Poremski, Erin, Sitarz, Rachel, Sturgeon, Nick, and Zhang, Yulong. (2014). *An Analysis of Cyber Attacks on the U.S. Financial System*. West Lafayette, IN: Center for Education and Research Information Assurance and Security, Purdue University. https://www.cerias.purdue.edu/assets/pdf/bibtex_archive/2014-3.pdf (accessed July 8, 2015).

Davidow, Bill. (2013, 23 August). "Productivity Tools for Cybercrime." *The Atlantic*. http://www.theatlantic.com/technology/archive/2013/08/productivity-tools-for-cybercrime/278974/ (accessed July 8, 2015).

Davies, Nick. (2014). *Hack Attack: The Inside Story of How the Truth Caught Up with Rupert Murdoch*. London, UK: Faber & Faber.

Décary-Hétu, David, and Dupont, Benoît. (2012). "The Social Network of Hackers." *Global Crime*, 13(3), 160–175.

DeMarco, Joseph V. (2001). "It's Not Just Fun and 'War Games'-Juveniles and Computer Crime." *United States Attorneys' Bulletin*, 49(3), 48–55.

Denning, Dorothy. (2001). "Cyberwarriors: Activists and Terrorists Turn to Cyberspace." *Harvard International Review*, 23(2), 70–75.

Denning, Dorothy. (2012). "Stuxnet: What Has Changed?" *Future Internet*, 4, 672–687.

Denning, Dorothy. (2014). "Framework and Principles for Active Cyber Defense." *Computers & Security*, 40, 108–113.

Denning, Dorothy, and Baugh, William E., Jr. "Hiding Crimes in Cyberspace" (2000).

In *Cybercrime: Law Enforcement, Security and Surveillance in the Information Age*, edited by Thomas and Loader, pp.105–131. London, UK: Routledge.

Dewey, Caitlin. (2014, 22 September). "There Are Now Officially a Billion Web Sites on the Internet (We Think)." *Washington Post*. http://www.washingtonpost.com/news/the-intersect/wp/2014/09/22/there-are-now-officially-a-billion-web-sites-on-the-internet-we-think/ (accessed July 8, 2015).

Edwards, O. (1995, 9 October). "Hackers from Hell." *Forbes*, p. 182.

Eichenwald, Kurt. (2005, 19 December). "Through His Webcam, a Boy Joins a Sordid Online World." *The New York Times*. http://www.nytimes.com/2005/12/19/national/19kids.ready.html?hp&ex=1135054800&en=5eb58e4d773204ee&ei=5094&partner=homepage (accessed July 8, 2015).

Electronic Privacy Information Center. (2003). United States v. Scarfo. Criminal No. 00-404 (D.N.J.). http://www.epic.org/crypto/scarfo.html (accessed July 8, 2015).

Electronic Privacy Information Center. (2005). *Total "Terrorism" Information Awareness (TIA)*. http://www.epic.org/privacy/profiling/tia/ (accessed July 8, 2015).

European Commission. (2012). *Special Eurobarometer 390: Cyber Security*. http://ec.europa.eu/public_opinion/archives/ebs/ebs_390_en.pdf (accessed July 8, 2015).

European Commission. (2013). *Special Eurobarometer 404: Cyber Security*. http://ec.europa.eu/public_opinion/archives/eb_special_419_400_en.htm (accessed July 8, 2015).

European Commission. (2015). *Special Eurobarometer 423: Cyber Security*. http://ec.europa.eu/public_opinion/archives/ebs/ebs_423_en.pdf (accessed July 8, 2015).

FBI. (2012). "Manhattan U.S. Attorney and FBI Assistant Director in Charge Announce 24 Arrests in Eight Countries as Part of International Cyber Crime Takedown." http://www.fbi.gov/newyork/press-releases/2012/manhattan-u.s.-attorney-and-fbi-assistant-director-in-charge-announce-24-arrests-in-eight-countries-as-part-of-international-cyber-crime-takedown (accessed July 8, 2015).

Feng, Bree. (2015, 20 January). "Among Snowden Leaks, Details of Chinese Cyberespionage." *The New York Times*. http://sinosphere.blogs.nytimes.com/2015/01/20/among-snowden-leaks-details-of-chinese-cyberespionage/?emc=edit_tnt_20150120&nlid=21079459&tntemail0=y (accessed July 8, 2015).

Foderaro, Lisa. (2010, 29 September). "Private Moment Made Public, Then a Fatal Jump." *The New York Times*. http://www.nytimes.com/2010/09/30/nyregion/30suicide.html (accessed 23 February 2014).

Freedom House. (2014). *Freedom on the Net.* https://freedomhouse.org/report-types/freedom-net (accessed July 8, 2015).

Gallagher, Ryan. (2014, 26 August). "The Surveillance Engine: How the NSA Built Its Own Secret Google." *The Intercept.* https://firstlook.org/theintercept/2014/08/25/icreach-nsa-cia-secret-google-crisscross-proton/ (accessed July 8, 2015).

Garfinkel, Simpson. (2011, 17 October). "The Criminal Cloud: Criminals Are Using Cloud Computing to Share Information and to Superpower Their Hacking Techniques." *MIT Technology Review.* http://www.technologyreview.com/news/425770/the-criminal-cloud/ (accessed July 8, 2015).

Geier, Eric. (2014, 13 January). "How to Rescue Your PC from Ransomware." *PC World.*http://www.pcworld.com/article/2084002/how-to-rescue-your-pc-from-ransomware.html (accessed July 8, 2015).

Gibbs, Samuel. (2014, 2 September). "FBI Investigating Hack of Naked Photos of Jennifer Lawrence and Others." *The Guardian.* http://www.theguardian.com/technology/2014/sep/02/fbi-investigating-hack-nude-celebrity-leak (accessed July 8, 2015).

Glenny, Misha. (2011). *Darkmarket: Cyberthieves, Cybercops and You.* London, UK: Bodley Head.

Global Voices. (2014). Vietnamese Government 'Opinion Shapers' Target Activist Facebook Pages. http://globalvoicesonline.org/2014/07/18/vietnamese-government-opinion-shapers-target-activist-facebook-pages/ (accessed July 8, 2015).

Gold, Jeffrey (1995, September 11) "Internet Sting Operation Nets Six Attempting to Sell Stolen Data" AP News Archive http://www.apnewsarchive.com/1995/Internet-Sting-Operation-Nets-Six-Attempting-to-Sell-Stolen-Data/id-22eda2455261dfb9133be63dcd196b9c/ (accessed July 7, 2015).

Goldstein, Joseph. (2013, 2 October). "Arrest in U.S. Shuts Down a Black Market for Narcotics." *The New York Times* http://www.nytimes.com/2013/10/03/nyregion/operator-of-online-market-for-illegal-drugs-is-charged-fbi-says.html. (accessed July 8, 2015).

Goldstein, Matthew. (2015, January 15). "Need Some Espionage Done? Hackers Are for Hire Online." *The New York Times.* http://dealbook.nytimes.com/2015/01/15/need-some-espionage-done-hackers-are-for-hire-online/ (accessed July 8, 2015).

Goldstone, David, and Shave, Betty-Ellen. (1998). "International Dimensions of Crimes in Cyberspace." *Fordham International Law Journal,* 22(5), 1924–1971.

Goncharov, Max. (2012). *Russian Underground 101.* http://www.trendmicro.com/cloud-content/us/pdfs/security-intelligence/white-papers/wp-russian-underground-101.pdf (accessed July 8, 2015).

Goodell, Jeff. (1996). *The Cyberthief and the Samurai.* New York, NY: Dell Publishing.

Goodman, Marc. (1997). "Why the Police Don't Care about Computer Crime." *Harvard Journal of Law and Technology,* 10(3), 465–494.

Goodman, Marc. (2001). "Making Computer Crime Count." *FBI Law Enforcement Bulletin.* https://www.hsdl.org/?view&did=442656 (accessed July 8, 2015).

Goodman, Marc. (2015). *Future Crime.* New York, NY: Random House.

Gordon, Lawrence A., Loeb, Martin P., Lucyshyn, William, and Richardson, Robert. (2005). *2005 CSI/FBI Computer Crime and Security Survey.* www.cpppe.umd.edu/Bookstore/Documents/2005CSISurvey.pdf (accessed July 8, 2015).

Gordon, Michael. (2014, 21 April). "Russia Displays a New Military Prowess in Ukraine's East." *The New York Times.* http://www.nytimes.com/2014/04/22/world/europe/new-prowess-for-russians.html?emc=edit_tnt_20140421&nlid=21079459&tntemail0=y# (accessed July 8, 2015).

Gordon, Gary R., Hosmer, Chet, Siedsma, Christine, and Rebovich, Don. (2002). *Assessing Technology, Methods, and Information for Committing and Combating Cybercrime.* Washington, DC: US Department of Justice.

Gough, Neil. (2013, September 5). "Chinese Official, a Symbol of Greed and Corruption, Is Sentenced." *The New York Times.* http://www.nytimes.com/2013/09/06/world/asia/yang-dacai-is-sentenced-in-china.html (accessed July 8, 2015).

Grabosky, Peter, and Smith, Russell G. (1998). *Crime in the Digital Age.* Sydney, Australia and New Brunswick, NJ: Federation Press/Transaction Publishers.

Grabosky, Peter, Smith, Russell G., and Dempsey, Gillian. (2001). *Electronic Theft: Unlawful Acquisition in Cyberspace.* Cambridge, UK: Cambridge University Press.

Grant, Anna, David, Fiona, and Grabosky, Peter. (2001). "The Commercial Sexual Exploitation of Children." *Current Issues in Criminal Justice,* 12(3), 269–287.

Greenberg, Andy. (2012). *This Machine Kills Secrets: How WikiLeakers, Cypherpunks, and Hacktivists Aim to Free the World's Information.* New York, NY: Dutton.

Greenwald, Glenn. (2014). *No Place to Hide: Edward Snowden, the NSA, and the U.S. Surveillance State.* New York, NY: Metropolitan Books.

Grossman, Lev. (2000, May 15). "Attack of the Love Bug." *Time,* p. 49.

Grubb, Ben. (2010, 8 September). "Film Industry Hires Cyber Hitmen to Take Down Internet Pirates." *Sydney Morning Herald.* http://www.smh.com.au/technology/technology-news/film-industry-hires-cyber-hitmen-to-take-down-internet-pirates-20100907-14ypv.html#ixzz205Bikun9 (accessed July 8, 2015).

The Guardian. (2012). "Social Media-Related Crime Reports Up 780% in Four Years." *The Guardian.* http://www.theguardian.com/media/2012/dec/27/social-media-crime-facebook-twitter (accessed July 8, 2015).

Hafner, Katie, and Markoff, John. (1991). *Cyberpunk: Outlaws and Hackers on the Electronic Frontier.* New York, NY: Simon and Schuster.

Hall, Louise. (2014, 25 July). "Jonathan Moylan Avoids Jail Term for Fake ANZ Media Release about Whitehaven Coal." *Sydney Morning Herald.* http://

www.smh.com.au/nsw/jonathan-moylan-avoids-jail-term-for-fake-anz-media-release-about-whitehaven-coal-20140725-zwwe7.html (accessed July 8, 2015).

Hansell, Saul. (2004). "When Software Fails to Stop Spam, It's Time to Bring In the Detectives." *The New York Times*. http://select.nytimes.com/gst/abstract.html?res=FA0A14FB345A0C728FDDAC0894DC404482 (accessed July 8, 2015).

Hardy, Kieran (2010). "Operation Titstorm: Hactivism or Cyber-Terrorism?" *UNSW Law Journal* 33(2), 474–502.

Harrell, Erika, and Langton, Lynn. (2013). *Victims of Identity Theft, 2012*. Washington, DC: Bureau of Justice Statistics.

Harris, Elizabeth. (2014, 5 May). "Faltering Target Parts Ways with Chief." *The New York Times*. http://www.nytimes.com/2014/05/06/business/target-chief-executive-resigns.html# (accessed July 8, 2015).

Henriques, Diana. (2011). *The Wizard of Lies: Bernie Madoff and the Death of Trust*. New York, NY: St Martin's Press.

Hilzenrath, David (1997, January 9) "Yale Student Pleads Guilty to Computer Fraud on AOL." *The Washington Post* http://www.washingtonpost.com/archive/business/1997/01/09/yale-student-pleads-guilty-to-computer-fraud-on-aol/e18906fc-d4e6-4333-adb3-1f6402369405/ (accessed July 8, 2015).

Holt, Thomas J. (2013). "Examining the Forces Shaping Cybercrime Markets Online." *Social Science Computer Review*, 31(2), 165–177.

Holt, Thomas J., Fitzgerald, Sarah, Bossler, Adam M., Chee, Grace, and Ng, Esther. (2014). "Assessing the Risk Factors of Cyber and Mobile Phone Bullying Victimization in a Nationally Representative Sample of Singapore Youth." *International Journal of Offender Therapy and Comparative Criminology*, 1–18. doi: 10.1177/0306624X14554852

Holt, Thomas J., Bossler, Adam M., and Seigfried-Spellar, Kathryn C. (2015). *Cybercrime and Digital Forensics*. London, UK: Routledge.

Huey, Laura, Nhan, Johnny, and Broll, Ryan. (2013). "Uppity Civilians and 'Cyber-Vigilantes': The Role of the General Public in Policing Cybercrime." *Criminology and Criminal Justice*, 13(1), 81–97.

Hutchings, Alice, and Holt, Thomas. (2014). "A Crime Script Analysis of the Online Stolen Data Market." *British Journal of Criminology*. doi:10.1093/bjc/azu106

International Telecommunications Union. (2014). "Key ICT Indicators for Developed and Developing Countries and the World (Totals and Penetration Rates)." Geneva, Switzerland: International Telecommunications Unions. http://www.itu.int/en/ITU-D/Statistics/Pages/default.aspx (accessed July 8, 2015).

Isaac, Mike. (2014, 2 September) "Nude Photos of Jennifer Lawrence Are Latest Front in Online Privacy Debate." *New York Times*. http://www.nytimes.com/2014/09/03/technology/trove-of-nude-photos-sparks-debate-over-online-behavior.html (accessed July 8, 2015).

Jacobs, Andrew. (2013, 5 February). "Chinese Blogger Thrives as Muckraker." *The New York Times*. http://www.nytimes.com/2013/02/06/world/asia/chinese-blogger-thrives-in-role-of-muckraker.html (accessed July 8, 2015).

Kates, Graham. (2012, 11 May). "Duped by Love." *The Crime Report*. http://www.thecrimereport.org/news/inside-criminal-justice/2012-05-duped-by-love (accessed July 8, 2015).

Kay, Russell. (2005, 4 April). "Biometric Authentication." *Computerworld*. http://www.computerworld.com/article/2556908/security0/biometric-authentication.html (accessed July 8, 2015).

Keelty, Mick. (2004, 29 November). *The Dark Side of Technology*. Presented to a Conference of the Australian Institute of Criminology, Melbourne. http://www.aic.gov.au/media_library/conferences/2004/keelty.pdf (accessed July 8, 2015).

Koops, Bert-Jaap, and Brenner, Susan W. (eds.). (2006). *Cybercrime and Jurisdiction: A Global Survey*. The Hague, The Netherlands: T.M.C. Asser Press.

Kowalski, Melanie. (2002). *Cyber-Crime: Issues Data Sources and Feasibility of Collecting Police-Reported Statistics*. Ottawa, ON: Statistics Canada. http://www5.statcan.gc.ca/olc-cel/olc.action?objId=85-558-X&objType=2&lang=en&limit=1 (accessed July 8, 2015).

Krone, T (2005a). *Phishing*. High Tech Crime Brief No. 9, Australian Institute of Criminology, Canberra. http://www.aic.gov.au/publications/current%20series/htcb/1-20/htcb009.html (accessed July 8, 2015.

Krone, T. (2005b). "Queensland Police Stings in Online Chat Rooms." *Trends & Issues in Crime and Criminal Justice*, 301 http://www.aic.gov.au/media_library/publications/tandi_pdf/tandi301.pdf (accessed July 8, 2015).

Landler, Mark, and Markoff, John. (2007, 29 May). "Digital Fears Emerge after Data Siege in Estonia." *The New York Times*. http://www.nytimes.com/2007/05/29/technology/29estonia.html?pagewanted=all (accessed July 8, 2015).

Lerner, Zach. (2014). "Microsoft the Botnet Hunter: The Role of Public Private Partnerships in Mitigating Botnets." *Harvard Journal of Law and Technology*, 28(1), 237–261.

Levy, Steven. (1984). *Hackers: Heroes of the Computer Revolution*. New York, NY: Penguin Books.

Liptak, Adam. (2006, 26 January). "In Case About Google's Secrets, Yours Are Safe." *The New York Times*. http://www.nytimes.com/2006/01/26/technology/26privacy.html?emc=eta1 (accessed July 8, 2015).

Majuca, Ruperto, and Kesan, Jay. (2009). *Hacking Back: Optimal Use of Self-Defense in Cyberspace*. Illinois Public Law Research Paper No. 08-20. http://papers.ssrn.com/sol3/papers.cfm?abstract_id=1363932 (accessed July 8, 2015).

Malcolm, John G. (2002, 20 November). "Special Briefing: Money Laundering and Payment Systems in Online Gambling." *World Online Gambling Law Report*. London, UK. https://www.google.com.au/webhp?sourceid=chrome-instant&ion=1&espv=2&ie=UTF-8#q=Special+Briefing%3A+Money+

Laundering+and+Payment+Systems+in+Online+Gambling (accessed July 8, 2015).

Malware Tips. (2015). *Your Computer Has Been Locked – Virus Removal Guide.* http://malwaretips.com/blogs/your-computer-has-been-locked-removal/ (accessed July 8, 2015).

Mandiant Intelligence Center. (2013). *APT1: Exposing One of China's Cyber Espionage Units.* http://intelreport.mandiant.com/Mandiant_APT1_Report.pdf (accessed July 8, 2015).

Martini, Ben, and Choo, K. K. Raymond. (2015). "An Integrated Conceptual Digital Forensic Framework for Cloud Computing." *Digital Investigation,* 9(2), 71–80.

Mazerolle, Lorraine, and Ransley, Janet. (2006). *Third Party Policing.* Cambridge, UK: Cambridge University Press.

Mazzetti, Mark. (2014, 23 April). "F.B.I. Informant Is Tied to Cyberattacks Abroad." *The New York Times.* http://www.nytimes.com/2014/04/24/world/fbi-informant-is-tied-to-cyberattacks-abroad.html?emc=edit_tnt_2 0140423&nlid=21079459&tntemail0=y# (accessed July 8, 2015).

Mazzetti, Mark, and Hulse, Carl. (2014, 31 July). "Inquiry by C.I.A. Affirms It Spied on Senate Panel." *The New York Times.* http://www.nytimes.com/2014/08/01/world/senate-intelligence-commitee-cia-interrogation-report.html (accessed July 8, 2015).

McCusker, R. (2005). "Spam: Nuisance or Menace, Prevention or Cure?" *Trends and Issues in Crime and Criminal Justice,* 294. http://www.aic.gov.au/publications/current%20series/tandi/281-300/tandi294.html (accessed July 8, 2015).

McKemmish, Rodney. (1999). "What is Forensic Computing?" *Trends and Issues in Crime and Criminal Justice,* 118. http://www.aic.gov.au/media_library/publications/tandi_pdf/tandi118.pdf(accessed July 8, 2015)

McNicol, Tony. (2005, 14 June). "Cyber War Grips Asia." *The Japan Times Online.* http://www.japantimes.co.jp/community/2005/06/14/issues/cyber-war-grips-asia/ (accessed July 8, 2015).

Miller, Greg, and Maharaj, Davan. (1999, 22 January). "N. Hollywood Man Charged in 1st Cyber-Stalking Case." *Los Angeles Times.* http://articles.latimes.com/1999/jan/22/news/mn-523 (accessed July 8, 2015).

Mills, Elinor. (2012, 30 June). "Cybercrime Moves to the Cloud." *CNet.* http://news.cnet.com/8301-1009_3-57464177-83/cybercrime-moves-to-the-cloud/ (accessed July 8, 2015).

Mitnick, Kevin. (2002). *The Art of Deception: Controlling the Human Element of Security.* Indianapolis, IN: Wiley Publishing.

Mitnick, Kevin, and Simon, William. (2005). *Art of Intrusion: The Real Stories behind the Exploits of Hackers, Intruders, & Deceivers.* Indianapolis, IN: Wiley Publishing.

Mitnick, Kevin, and Simon, William. (2011). *Ghost in the Wires: My Adventures as the World's Most Wanted Hacker.* Boston, MA: Little, Brown.

Mobithinking. (2014). *Global Mobile Statistics 2014 Part A: Mobile Subscribers; Handset Market Share; Mobile Operators*. http://mobithinking.com/mobile-marketing-tools/latest-mobile-stats/a#uniquesubscribers (accessed 14 May 2014).

Morton, Tom. (2004). *Mutating Mobiles*. Background Briefing ABC Radio National. http://www.abc.net.au/radionational/programs/backgroundbriefing/mutating-mobiles/3408828 (accessed July 8, 2015).

Moses, Asher. (2010, 10 February). "Operation Titstorm: Hackers Bring Down Government Websites." *Sydney Morning Herald*. http://www.smh.com.au/technology/technology-news/operation-titstorm-hackers-bring-down-government-websites-20100210-nqku.html (accessed July 8, 2015).

Motion Picture Association (MPA). (2003a). *Motion Picture Association (MPA) Announces Expeditious Resolution of Two Landmark Civil Action Proceedings Concerning DVD Piracy in China*. Encino, CA/Hong Kong: MPA.

Motion Picture Association (MPA). (2003b). *Motion Picture Association (MPA) Announces The Successful Resolution of Six Civil Action Proceedings Concerning DVD Piracy in Shanghai*. Encino, CA/Hong Kong: MPA.

Motivans, Mark and Kyckelhahn, Tracey. (2007). *Federal Prosecution of Child Sex Exploitation Offenders, 2006*. Washington, DC: Bureau of Justice Statistics.

Mozur, Paul, Perlroth, Nicole, and Chen, Brian. (2014, 21 October). "Apple's iCloud Storage Service Is Aim of Attack in China." *The New York Times*. http://www.nytimes.com/2014/10/22/technology/china-attack-aims-at-apple-icloud-storage-service.html (accessed July 8, 2015).

Nakashima, Ellen. (2015, 2 April). "U.S. Establishes Sanctions Program to Combat Cyberattacks, Cyberspying." *The Washington Post*. http://www.washingtonpost.com/world/national-security/us-to-establish-sanctions-program-to-combat-cyberattacks-cyberspying/2015/03/31/7f563474-d7dc-11e4-ba28-f2a685dc7f89_story.html (accessed July 8, 2015).

Nasheri, Hedieh. (2005). *Corporate Espionage and Industrial Spying*. Cambridge, UK: Cambridge University Press.

Neumann, Peter G. (1996). "CIA Disconnects Home Page after Being Hacked." *The Risks Digest*, 18, 49. http://catless.ncl.ac.uk/Risks/18.49.html#subj2 (accessed July 8, 2015).

The New York Times. (2005, 13 December). "Australian Mobs Attack People Believed to Be of Arab Descent". http://www.nytimes.com/2005/12/13/world/asia/australian-mobs-attack-people-believed-to-be-of-arab-descent.html (accessed July 8, 2015).

Newman, Graeme R., and Clarke, Ronald V. (2003). *Superhighway Robbery: Preventing e-Commerce Crime*. Devon, UK: Willan Publishing.

Nhan, Johnny. (2010). *Policing Cyberspace: A Structural and Cultural Analysis*. El Paso TX: LFB Scholarly Publishing.

Nobles, Matt R., Reyns, Bradford W., Fox, Kathleen A., and Fisher, Bonnie S. (2014).
"Protection Against Pursuit: A Conceptual and Empirical Comparison of Cyberstalking and Stalking Victimization Among a National Sample" Justice Quarterly, 31(6), 986–1014.

Office for National Statistics (UK). (2014). *Work to Extend the Crime Survey for England and Wales to Include Fraud and Cyber-Crime.* http://www.ons.gov.uk/ons/guide-method/method-quality/specific/crime-statistics-methodology/methodological-notes/index.html (accessed July 8, 2015).

Oliver, John, Cheng, Sandra, Manly, Lala, Zhu, Joey, Dela Paz, Roland, Sioting, Sabrina, and Leopando, Jonathan. (2012). *Blackhole Exploit Kit: A Spam Campaign, Not a Series of Individual Spam Runs.* http://www.trendmicro.com.au/cloud-content/us/pdfs/security-intelligence/white-papers/wp_blackhole-exploit-kit.pdf (accessed July 8, 2015).

Olson, Parmy. (2012). *We Are Anonymous: Inside the Hacker World of LulzSec, Anonymous, and the Global Cyber Insurgency.* New York, NY: Little, Brown.

Orwell, George. (1951). *1984.* London, UK: Secker & Warburg.

Painter, Christopher. (2001). "Supervised Release and Probation Restrictions in Hacker Cases." *US Attorneys Bulletin*, 49, 2, 43-48

Parker, Donn B. (1976). *Crime by Computer.* New York, NY: Charles Scribner's Sons.

Perlroth, Nicole. (2012a, 12 June). "After Rapes Involving Children, Skout, a Flirting App, Bans Minors." *The New York Times.* http://bits.blogs.nytimes.com/2012/06/12/after-rapes-involving-children-skout-a-flirting-app-faces-crisis/?hp (accessed July 8, 2015).

Perlroth, Nicole. (2012b, 5 December). "For PC Virus Victims, Pay or Else." *The New York Times.* http://www.nytimes.com/2012/12/06/technology/ransomware-is-expanding-in-the-united-states.html (accessed July 8, 2015).

Perlroth, Nicole. (2014, 8 April). "Experts Find a Door Ajar in an Internet Security Method Thought Safe." *The New York Times.* http://bits.blogs.nytimes.com/2014/04/08/flaw-found-in-key-method-for-protecting-data-on-the-internet/?emc=edit_tnt_20140408&nlid=21079459&tntemail0=y# (accessed July 8 2015).

Perlroth, Nicole, and Sanger, David. (2013, 13 July). "Nations Buying as Hackers Sell Flaws in Computer Code." *The New York Times.* http://www.nytimes.com/2013/07/14/world/europe/nations-buying-as-hackers-sell-computer-flaws.html?pagewanted=all (accessed 12 August 2013).

Perlroth, Nicole, and Wortham, Jenna. (2014, 3 April). "Tech Start-Ups Are Targets of Ransom Cyberattacks." *The New York Times.* http://bits.blogs.nytimes.com/2014/04/03/tech-start-ups-are-targets-of-ransom-cyberattacks/# (accessed July 8, 2015).

Pontell, Henry N., and Rosoff, Stephen M. (2009). "White-Collar Delinquency." *Crime Law and Social Change*, 51(1), 147–162.

Power, Richard. (2000). *Tangled Web: Tales of Digital Crime from the Shadows of Cyberspace*. Indianapolis, IN: Que Publishers.

Raghavan, Sudarsan. (2014, 9 January). "Somalia's al-Shabab Militia Bans Internet." *Washington Post*. http://www.washingtonpost.com/world/somalias-al-shabab-militia-bans-internet/2014/01/09/7c288bdc-7953-11e3-a647-a19deaf575b3_story.html (accessed July 8, 2015).

Rantala, Ramona R. (2008). *Cybercrime Against Businesses, 2005*. Washington, DC: Bureau of Justice Statistics.

Reuters. (2014, 20 August). "U.S. Hospital Breach Biggest Yet to Exploit Heartbleed Bug: Expert." *The New York Times*. http://www.nytimes.com/reuters/2014/08/20/technology/20reuters-community-health-cybersecurity.html (accessed July 8, 2015).

Reuters Canada. (2014). *NSA Infiltrates Servers of China Telecom Giant Huawei: Report*. http://ca.reuters.com/article/businessNews/idCABREA2L0PD20140322?pageNumber=1&virtualBrandChannel=0 (accessed July 8, 2014).

Rheingold, Howard. (2002). *Smart Mobs: The Next Social Revolution*. Cambridge, MA: Perseus Books.

Richtel, Matt. (2005, 10 December). "Live Tracking of Mobile Phones Prompts Court Fights on Privacy." *The New York Times*. http://www.nytimes.com/2005/12/10/technology/live-tracking-of-mobile-phones-prompts-court-fights-on-privacy.html (accessed July 8, 2015).

Risen, James, and Lichtblau, Eric. (2005, 6 December). "Bush Lets U.S. Spy on Callers without Courts." *The New York Times*, p. 1. http://www.nytimes.com/2005/12/16/politics/bush-lets-us-spy-on-callers-without-courts.html (accessed July 8, 2015)

Romero, Simon. (2013, 9 September). "N.S.A. Spied on Brazilian Oil Company, Report Says." *The New York Times*. http://www.nytimes.com/2013/09/09/world/americas/nsa-spied-on-brazilian-oil-company-report-says.html (accessed July 8, 2015).

Rosoff, Stephen M., Pontell, Henry N., and Tillman, Robert H. (1998). *Profit without Honor: White-Collar Crime and the Looting of America*. Upper-Saddle River, NJ: Prentice Hall.

Rustad, Michael. (2001). "Private Enforcement of Cybercrime on the Electronic Frontier." *Southern California Interdisciplinary Law Journal*, 11(1), 63–116.

Sanger, David. (2012). *Confront and Conceal: Obama's Secret Wars and Surprising Use of American Power*. New York, NY: Crown Publishers.

Sanger, David. (2013, 31 August). "Budget Documents Detail Extent of U.S. Cyberoperations." *The New York Times*. http://www.nytimes.com/2013/09/01/world/americas/documents-detail-cyberoperations-by-us.html?emc=edit_tnt_20130831&tntemail0=y (accessed July 8, 2015).

Sanger, David. (2014, 20 May). "Fine Line Seen in U.S. Spying on Companies." *The New York Times*. http://www.nytimes.com/2014/05/21/business/us-snooping-on-companies-cited-by-china.html (accessed July 8, 2015).

Sanger, David. (2015, 22 February). "Document Reveals Growth of Cyberwarfare Between the U.S. and Iran." *The New York Times.* http://www.nytimes.com/2015/02/23/us/document-reveals-growth-of-cyberwarfare-between-the-us-and-iran.html (accessed July 8, 2015).

Sanger, David, Barboza, David, and Perlroth, Nicole (2013, 18 February) "Chinese Army Unit Is Seen as Tied to Hacking Against U.S." *The New York Times* http://www.nytimes.com/2013/02/19/technology/chinas-army-is-seen-as-tied-to-hacking-against-us.html?_r=0 (accessed July 8, 2015).

Sanger, David, and Fackler, Martin. (2015, 18 January). "N.S.A. Breached North Korean Networks Before Sony Attack, Officials Say." *The New York Times.* http://www.nytimes.com/2015/01/19/world/asia/nsa-tapped-into-north-korean-networks-before-sony-attack-officials-say.html (accessed July 8, 2015).

Sanger, David, and Perlroth, Nicole. (2015a, 14 February). "Bank Hackers Steal Millions via Malware." *The New York Times.* http://www.nytimes.com/2015/02/15/world/bank-hackers-steal-millions-via-malware.html?_r=0 (accessed July 8, 2015).

Sanger, David, and Perlroth, Nicole. (2015b, 16 February). "U.S. Embedded Spyware Overseas, Report Claims." *The New York Times.* http://www.nytimes.com/2015/02/17/technology/spyware-embedded-by-us-in-foreign-networks-security-firm-says.html?&hp&action=click&pgtype=Homepage&module=first-column-region&region=top-news&WT.nav=top-news (accessed July 8, 2015).

Sanger, David, Perlroth, Nicole, and Shear, Michael. (2015, 21 June). "Attack Gave Chinese Hackers Privileged Access to U.S. Systems" *The New York Times.* http://www.nytimes.com/2015/06/21/us/attack-gave-chinese-hackers-privileged-access-to-us-systems.html (accesssed July 8, 2015),

Schiesel, Seth. (2004, 17 June). "Turning the Tables on E-Mail Swindlers." *The New York Times.* http://www.nytimes.com/2004/06/17/technology/circuits/17hoax.html?ex=1402891200&en=c41168a8fa42945f&ei=5007&partner=USERLAND (accessed July 8, 2015).

Schmitt, Michael. (ed.). (2013). *Tallinn Manual on the International Law Applicable to Cyber Warfare.* Cambridge, UK: Cambridge University Press.

Schneider, Jacqueline. (2003). "Hiding in Plain Sight: An Exploration of the Illegal(?) Activities of a Drugs Newsgroup." *The Howard Journal,* 42(4), 374–389.

Schroeder, Steve. (2012). *The Lure: The True Story of How the Department of Justice Brought Down Two of The World's Most Dangerous Cyber Criminals.* Boston, MA: Course Technology.

Schwartz, John. (2004, 28 March). "Frontier Justice; On the Web, Vengeance Is Mine (and Mine)." *The New York Times.* http://www.nytimes.com/2004/03/28/weekinreview/ideas-trends-frontier-justice-on-the-web-vengeance-is-mine-and-mine.html?pagewanted=all&src=pm (accessed July 8, 2015).

Scott, Mark. (2015, 20 February). "Chip Maker to Investigate Claims of Hacking by N.S.A. and British Spy Agencies." *The New York Times.* http://www.

nytimes.com/2015/02/21/world/europe/chip-maker-to-investigate-claims-of-hacking-by-nsa-and-british-spy-agencies.html?emc=edit_tnt_2 0150220&nlid=21079459&tntemail0=y (accessed July 8, 2015).

Seltzer, William, and Anderson, Margo. (2001). "The Dark Side of Numbers: The Role of Population Data Systems in Human Rights Abuses." *Social Research*, 68(2), 481–414.

Shane, Scott, and Hubbard, Ben. (2014, 30 August). "ISIS Displaying a Deft Command of Varied Media." *The New York Times*. http://www.nytimes.com/2014/08/31/world/middleeast/isis-displaying-a-deft-command-of-varied-media.html?_r=0 (accessed July 8, 2015).

Shapiro, Fred. (1987). "Etymology of the Computer Bug: History and Folklore." *American Speech*, 62(4), 376–378.

Shimomura, Tsutomu, and Markoff, John. (1996). *Takedown: The Pursuit and Capture of Kevin Mitnick, America's Most Wanted Computer Outlaws—by the Man Who Did It.* New York, NY: Hyperion Books.

Sieber, U. (1998). *Legal Aspects of Computer-Related Crime in the Information Society.* COMCRIME Study prepared for the European Commission. http://www.oas.org/juridico/english/COMCRIME%20Study.pdf (accessed July 8, 2015).

Silva, Sergio, Silva, Rodrigo, Pinto, Raquel, and Salles, Ronaldo (2013) "Botnets: A survey" *Computer Networks*, 57, 2, 378-403.

Sipress, A. (2004, December 14). An Indonesian's Prison Memoir Takes Holy War Into Cyberspace: In Sign of New Threat, Militant Offers Tips on Credit Card Fraud. *Washington Post*. http://www.washingtonpost.com/wp-dyn/articles/A62095-2004Dec13.html (accessed July 8, 2015)

Slatalla, Michelle, and Quittner, Joshua. (1995). *Masters of Deception: The Gang That Ruled Cyberspace.* New York, NY: Harper Collins.

Smith, Bruce. (2005). "Hacking, Poaching and Counterattacking: Digital Counterstrikes and the Contours of Self-Help." *Journal of Law, Economics and Policy*, 1(1), 171–195.

Smith, Russell G., Grabosky, Peter, and Urbas, Gregor. (2004). *Cybercriminals on Trial.* Cambridge, UK: Cambridge University Press.

Steinhauer, Jennifer. (2008, 26 November). "Verdict in MySpace Suicide Case." *The New York Times*. http://www.nytimes.com/2008/11/27/us/27myspace.html (accessed July 8, 2015).

Sterling, Bruce. (1992). *The Hacker Crackdown.* New York, NY: Bantam Books.

Stoll, Clifford. (1989). *The Cuckoo's Egg.* New York, NY: Pocket Books.

Sussmann, Michael A. (1999). "The Critical Challenges from International High tech and Computer Related Crime at the Millennium." *Duke Journal of Comparative and International Law*, 9, 451–489.

Thomas, Douglas, and Loader, Brian D. (eds.). (2000). *Cybercrime.* London, UK: Routledge.

Thompson, Clive. (2004, 8 February). "The Virus Underground." *The New York Times Magazine.* http://www.nytimes.com/2004/02/08/magazine/08WORMS .html (accessed July 8, 2015).

Thompson, Trevor. (2009). "Terrorizing the Technological Neighborhood Watch: The Alienation and Deterrence of the 'White Hats' under the CFAA." *Florida State University Law Review*, 36, 537–584.

Tusikov, Natasha. (2015). "Project Goliath: Internet Intermediaries and the Online Regulation of Intellectual Property". https://www.academia.edu/ 10619862/Project_Goliath_Internet_Intermediaries_and_the_Online_ Regulation_of_Intellectual_Property (accessed July 8, 2015).

United Kingdom, Biometrics Working Group. (2006). *Use of Biometrics for Identification: Advice on Product Selection.* http://www.idsysgroup.com/files/ Biometrics%20Advice.pdf (accessed July 8, 2015).

United Nations Office on Drugs and Crime (UNODC). (2013). *Comprehensive Study on Cybercrime Draft-2013.* Vienna, Austria: UNODC.

Urbas, Gregor. (2006a). "Criminalising Computer Misconduct: Some Legal and Philosophical Problems." *Asia Pacific Law Review*, 14(6), 95–121.

Urbas, Gregor. (2006b). "Cross-National Investigation and Prosecution of Intellectual Property Crimes: The Example of 'Operation Buccaneer.'" *Crime, Law and Social Change*, 46(4-5), 207–221.

Urbas, Gregor. (2010). "Protecting Children from Online Predators: The Use of Covert Investigation Techniques by Law Enforcement." *Journal of Contemporary Criminal Justice*, 26(4), 410–425.

US Department of Homeland Security. (2011). *Secretary Napolitano and Attorney General Holder Announce Largest U.S. Prosecution of International Criminal Network Organized to Sexually Exploit Children.* http://www.dhs.gov/ news/2011/08/03/secretary-napolitano-and-attorney-general-holder-announce-largest-us-prosecution (accessed July 8, 2015).

US Department of Justice. (n.d.). *Searching and Seizing Computers and Obtaining Electronic Evidence in Criminal Investigations.* http://www.justice.gov/criminal/cybercrime/documents.html (accessed July 8, 2015).

US Department of Justice. (1998). *Israeli Citizen Arrested in Israel for Hacking United States and Israeli Government Computers.* http://www.justice.gov/archive/opa/pr/1998/March/125.htm.html (accessed July 8, 2015).

US Department of Justice. (2001). *Computer Security Expert Sentenced to 27 Months' Imprisonment for Computer Hacking and Electronic Eavesdropping.* http://www.cybercrime.gov/OquendoSent.htm (accessed 2 January 2006).

US Department of Justice. (2002). *Six Defendants Sentenced in $16 Million Bogus Investment Scheme Marketed Over Internet.* http://www.justice.gov/archive/ criminal/cybercrime/press-releases/2002/guastella_martins.htm (accessed July 8, 2015).

US Department of Justice. (2003). *Defendant Indicted in Connection with Operating Illegal Internet Software Piracy Group.* http://www.justice.gov/archive/

criminal/cybercrime/press-releases/2003/griffithsIndict.htm (accessed July 8, 2015).

US Department of Justice. (2004a). *Six Internet Fraudsters Indicted in International Conspiracy To Steal More Than $10 Million From World's Largest Technology Distributor.* http://www.justice.gov/archive/criminal/cybercrime/press-releases/2004/mateiasIndict.htm (accessed July 8, 2015)).

US Department of Justice. (2004b). *Former Employee of a Massachusetts High-Technology Firm Charged With Computer Hacking.* http://www.justice.gov/archive/criminal/cybercrime/press-releases/2004/angleCharged.htm (accessed July 8, 2015).

US Department of Justice. (2004c). *Hacker Sentenced to Prison for Breaking into Lowe's Companies' Computers with Intent to Steal Credit Card Information.* http://www.justice.gov/archive/criminal/cybercrime/press-releases/2004/salcedoSent.htm (accessed July 8, 2015).

US Department of Justice. (2004d). *Forensic Examination of Digital Evidence: A Guide for Law Enforcement.* Washington, DC: National Institute of Justice. https://www.ncjrs.gov/pdffiles1/nij/199408.pdf (accessed July 8, 2015).

US Department of Justice. (2005a). *Creator and Four Users of Loverspy Spyware Program Indicted.* http://www.justice.gov/archive/criminal/cybercrime/press-releases/2005/perezIndict.htm (accessed July 8, 2015).

US Department of Justice. (2005b). *Justice Department Announces Conviction of Florida Man Accused of Massive Data Theft from Acxiom, Inc.* http://www.justice.gov/archive/criminal/cybercrime/press-releases/2005/levineConvict.htm (accessed July 8, 2015).

US Department of Justice. (2005c). *Disgruntled Phillies Fan/Spammer Sent to Prison for Four Years.* http://www.justice.gov/archive/criminal/cybercrime/press-releases/2005/carlsonSent.htm (accessed July 8, 2015).

US Department of Justice. (2005d). *Massachusetts Teen Convicted for Hacking into Internet and Telephone Service Providers and Making Bomb Threats to High Schools in Massachusetts and Florida.* Press Release, US Attorney's Office, District of Massachusetts. http://www.justice.gov/archive/criminal/cybercrime/press-releases/2005/juvenileSentboston.htm (accessed July 8, 2015).

US Department of Justice. (2005e). *Operation Buccaneer.* http://www.usdoj.gov/criminal/cybercrime/ob/OBMain.htm (accessed 23 December 2005); http://web.archive.org/web/20110722172136/http://www.cybercrime.gov/ob/OBMain.htm (accessed July 8, 2015).

US Department of Justice. (2009). *Virginia Software Writer Pleads Guilty to Aiding and Abetting Detroit Spam Conspiracy.* http://www.justice.gov/opa/pr/virginia-software-writer-pleads-guilty-aiding-and-abetting-detroit-spam-conspiracy (accessed 23 January 2015).

US Department of Justice. (2013). *Members of New York Cell of Cybercrime Organization Plead Guilty in $45 Million Cybercrime Campaign.* http://www.justice.gov/usao/nye/pr/2013/2013nov12.html (accessed July 8, 2015).

US Department of Justice. (2014a). *Searching and Seizing Computers and Obtaining Electronic Evidence in Criminal Investigations.* http://www.justice.gov/sites/default/files/criminal-ccips/legacy/2015/01/14/ssmanual2009.pdf (accessed July 8, 2015).

US Department of Justice. (2014b). *More Than 400 .Onion Addresses, Including Dozens of 'Dark Market' Sites, Targeted as Part of Global Enforcement Action on Tor Network.* http://www.justice.gov/opa/pr/more-400-onion-addresses-including-dozens-dark-market-sites-targeted-part-global-enforcement (accessed July 8, 2015).

US Department of Justice. (2014c). *Dozens of Online "Dark Markets" Seized Pursuant to Forfeiture Complaint Filed in Manhattan Federal Court in Conjunction with the Arrest of the Operator of Silk Road 2.0.* http://www.justice.gov/usao/nys/pressreleases/November14/DarkMarketTakedown.php (accessed July 8, 2015).

US Department of Justice. (n.d.). *Operation Delego Court Documents.* http://www.justice.gov/opa/operation-delego-court-documents (accessed July 8, 2015).

US Federal Bureau of Investigation. (2003). *Carnivore DCS 1000 Report to Congress.* http://www.epic.org/privacy/carnivore/2003_report.pdf (accessed July 8, 2015).

US General Accounting Office. (2004). *Data Mining: Federal Efforts Cover a Wide Range of Uses.* Washington, DC: USGAO. http://www.epic.org/privacy/profiling/gao_dm_rpt.pdf (accessed July 8, 2015).

US Securities and Exchange Commission. (2000). *In the Matter of Jonathan G. Lebed.* http://www.sec.gov/litigation/admin/33-7891.htm (accessed July 8, 2015).

van Kempen, Linda (2014, 20 May) "Alexandra man uses Facebook to arrange fight with teens" *Otago Daily Times* http://www.odt.co.nz/regions/central-otago/302864/warning-over-fights-arranged-social-media (accessed July 8, 2015).

Vaughan, Diane. (1983). *Controlling Unlawful Organizational Behavior: Social Structure and Corporate Misconduct.* Chicago, IL: University of Chicago Press.

Vaughan-Nichols, Steven. (2014, 13 February). "Worst DDoS Attack of All Time Hits French Site." *ZD News.* http://www.zdnet.com/article/worst-ddos-attack-of-all-time-hits-french-site/ (accessed July 8, 2015).

Verini, James. (2010, 10 November). "The Great Cyberheist." *The New York Times* http://www.nytimes.com/2010/11/14/magazine/14Hacker-t.html?pagewanted=all (accessed July 8, 2015).

Vijayan, Jaikumar. (2013, 20 August). "Attackers Turning to Legit Cloud Services Firms to Plant Malware." *Computerworld.* http://www.computerworld.com/s/article/9241324/Attackers_turning_to_legit_cloud_services_firms_to_plant_malware (accessed July 8, 2015).

Virgillito, Dan. (2014). "70% of Young Iranians Surf the Web Illegally." *VPN Creative* https://vpncreative.net/2014/09/19/70-young-iranians-surf-illegally/ (accessed 8 July 2015).

Wakefield, Jane. (2014, 7 November). "Huge Raid to Shut Down 400-Plus Dark Net Sites." *BBC News.* http://www.bbc.com/news/technology-29950946 (accessed 8 July 2015).

Warren, Samuel, and Brandeis, Louis. (1890). "The Right to Privacy." *Harvard Law Review,* 4(5), 193–220.

Weiser, Benjamin. (2014, 27 May). "Hacker Who Helped Disrupt Cyberattacks Is Allowed to Walk Free." *The New York Times.* http://www.nytimes.com/2014/05/28/nyregion/hacker-who-helped-disrupt-cyberattacks-is-allowed-to-walk-free.html# (accessed July 8, 2015).

The White House. (2003). *The National Strategy to Secure Cyberspace.* Washington, DC: The White House. https://www.us-cert.gov/sites/default/files/publications/cyberspace_strategy.pdf (accessed July 8, 2015).

Wible, Brent. (2003). "A Site Where Hackers are Welcome: Using Hack-in Contests to Shape Preferences and Deter Computer Crime." *Yale Law Journal,* 112, 1577–1623.

Williams, Matthew L. (2015). "Guardians upon High: An Application of Routine Activities Theory to Online Identity Theft in Europe at the Country and Individual Level." *British Journal of Criminology.* doi: 10.1093/bjc/azv011. First published online: April 27, 2015

Wilson, Clay. (2005). Computer Attack and Cyberterrorism: Vulnerabilities and Policy Issues for Congress. Congressional Research Service, Library of Congress, Washington, DC. http://fas.org/irp/crs/RL32114.pdf (accessed July 8, 2015).

Wilson, Clay. (2007). *Information Operations, Electronic Warfare, and Cyberwar: Capabilities and Related Policy Issues.* Congressional Research Service, Library of Congress, Washington, DC. https://www.fas.org/sgp/crs/natsec/RL31787.pdf (accessed July 8, 2015).

Wines, Michael. (2011, 10 June). "Nearly 600 Arrested in Asian Swindling Ring." *The New York Times.* http://www.nytimes.com/2011/06/11/world/asia/11taiwan.html (accessed July 8, 2015).

Wong, Edward. (2014, 23 May). "U.S. Case Offers Glimpse into China's Hacker Army." *The New York Times.* http://www.nytimes.com/2014/05/23/world/asia/us-case-offers-glimpse-into-chinas-hacker-army.html?hp# (accessed July 8, 2015).

Wood, Molly. (2015, 7 January). "CES: Security Risks from the Smart Home." *The New York Times.* http://www.nytimes.com/2015/01/08/technology/personaltech/ces-security-risks-from-the-smart-home.html?emc=edit_tnt_20150107&nlid=21079459&tntemail0=y (accessed July 8, 2015).

Zetter, Kim. (2014). *Countdown to Zero Day: Stuxnet and the World's First Digital Weapon.* New York, NY: Crown Publishers.

USEFUL WEBSITES RELATING TO CYBERCRIME

Benoît Dupont's Home Page
(mostly in French)
http://www.benoitdupont.net/

Berkman Center for Internet and
Society, Harvard University
https://cyber.law.harvard.edu/

Center for Internet and Society,
Stanford University
https://cyberlaw.stanford.edu/

Computer Crime Research
Center (Ukraine)
http://www.crime-research.org/

Cyberangels (United States)
http://www.cyberangels.org/

Cyber-Rights and
Cyber-Liberties (UK)
http://www.cyber-rights.org/

Dorothy Denning's Home Page
http://faculty.nps.edu/dedennin/

Electronic Frontier Foundation
http://www.eff.org/

Electronic Privacy
Information Center
http://www.epic.org

European Union Forum on
Cybercrime
http://cybercrime-forum.jrc.it/
default/

Examples of Hacked Web Pages
http://www.2600.com/hacked_
pages/old_archives.html
(*Caution*: readers are urged not to
emulate the exploits depicted
therein, as such a course of action
is likely to entail the commission
of a criminal offence.)

Freedom House Annual Report:
Freedom on the Net
https://freedomhouse.org/report-
types/freedom-net

Gene Spafford's Home Page
http://homes.cerias.purdue.
edu/%7Espaf/index.html

Infowar.Com
http://www.infowar.com

The Intercept
https://firstlook.org/theintercept/

Institute for Information
Infrastructure Protection
http://www.thei3p.org

Judge Stein Schjolberg's
Cybercrime Law Webpage
http://www.cybercrimelaw.net/
Cybercrimelaw.html

Kevin Mitnick's Home Page
https://www.mitnicksecurity.com/

Lawrence Lessig's Home Page
http://www.lessig.org

Marc Goodman's Home Page
http://www.marcgoodman.net/

National White Collar Crime
Center (US)
https://www.nw3c.org/

Netsafe (New Zealand)
http://www.netsafe.org.nz/

Orin Kerr's Home Page
http://www.law.gwu.edu/
Faculty/Profile.aspx?id=3568

Oxford Internet Institute
http://www.oii.ox.ac.uk/

US Department of Justice, Child
Exploitation and Obscenity
Section
http://www.justice.gov/
criminal-ceos

Computer Crime and Intellectual
Property Section
http://www.cybercrime.gov/
index.html

US Federal Bureau of
Investigation, Cyber
Investigations
http://www.fbi.gov/ipr/

Virtual Forum Against
Cybercrime
https://www.cybercrimeforum.org/

Wired Magazine
http://www.wired.com/

ADDITIONAL READING

Gasser, Urs, Zittrain, Jonathan, Faris, Robert, Jones, Rebekah Heacock (2014). *Internet Monitor 2014: Reflections on the Digital World: Platforms, Policy, Privacy, and Public Discourse*. The Berkman Center for Internet & Society Research Publication Series: Research Publication No. 2014-17. http://cyber.law.harvard.edu/publications/2014/reflections_on_the_ digital_world

Holt, Thomas, Bossler, Adam, and Seigfried-Spellar, Kathryn (2015). *Cybercrime and Digital Forensics: An Introduction*. New York: Routledge.

INDEX

Access codes, 13
Access to computers, 55–57
  control strategies, 123–124
Addiction to computers (as defense),
  110–111
Advance-fee fraud letters, 19–20, 36,
  61, 129
  nonreporting of, 61
  private citizens' actions, 127–129
America Online
  criminal warrants, 89–100
  Anonymous, 4, 97
Anonymous e-mail, 32
Anti-phishing Working Group, 125
Antivirus software, 34, 58, 66
Ardita, Julio Cesar ("Griton"), 10
ATM fraud. 28, 98, 131
Auctions online
  complaints, 58
  fraud, 25–26
  security enforcement. 125–127
Australian High Tech Crime Centre
  (AHTCC), 108
Australian Institute of Criminology, 63, 88

Backups, double copies of, 93
Bill of Rights, (U.S.), 93, 129–130
Biometric authentication, techniques
  listed, 123
Blue boxes, 14
Botnet (abbreviation of robot network),
  32, 61, 81, 87
  in denial of service attacks, 34, 35
Brandeis, Louis, 87
British Crime Survey (BCS), 65
Bullying, 43
Bush, George W., 18, 46
Business Software Alliance, 70

Calling card number theft,
  15Cannibalism, 45
CAN SPAM Act (2003), 133
Canada, 17, 35, 49
Cap'n Crunch, 14
Carnivore (DCS 1000) network collection
  technlogies, 89
Casinos, online, 41
Categories of computer crime, 8–12
Celebrity (or notoriety) motive, 57
Cellular phones, 12–13
CENTCOM (See United States Central
  Command)
Center for Online and Internet
  Addiction, 110
Child pornography
  background, 13, 16
  commercialization, 80
  defenses, 111, 112
  evidence of knowledge and intent, 112
  fantasy defense, 112
  legislation, 6, 7
  motives, 56, 57, 84
  offender profiles, 72
  offensive content, 41–42
  online investigations, 96
  Operation Artus, 107
  Operation Cathedral, 107
  Operation Falcon, 108
  private citizens against, 95, 127–128
  requirement to assist
    governments, 125–127
  sentencing, 16, 111
China, 17, 18, 41, 72, 77, 102, 109, 128
CIA (Central Intelligence Agency), 18,
  30, 46
Civil remedies, 126, 127
  spam violations, 134

Civility, culture of cyberspace, 121
Cloud computing, 105-106
Code Red Virus, 76
Commercialization, 80–82
Competition, 18
Computer Emergency Readiness Team
    (US-CERT), 126
Computer Emergency Response Team
    (CERT), 126
Computer Fraud and Abuse Act, 11, 43
Computer-mediated communications
    illegal interception of, 12–13
Computer-related crime. *See* Electronic
    crime
Computers
    as instruments, 8
    as targets, 8
Conspiracies, criminal, 4, 15, 16, 17
Content regulation, 7
    problems with, 42
Copyright protection
    Operation Buccaneer, 107
    piracy and, 19
    security enforcement and, 97
Corporate fraud
    information systems and, 4
Corporate intelligence collection, 18–19
Costs of computer crime, 70
Computer Hacking and Intellectual
    Property (CHIP) Attorney, 110
Computer Security Institute, 65
Council of Europe Cybercrime
    Convention, 132
Counter-hackers, 128
Counter-scammers, 129
Counterfeiting. *See also* Websites,
    counterfeiting
    prosecution, 116
    scanning technology, 29
Crackers, 5
Credit cards
    online fraud, 72
    theft of card details, 15–16
    wireless technology, 15
Crime in the Digital Age (Grabosky and
    Smith), 2
Crime scenes, 91
Criminal havens, 75

Criminal procedure, law of
    adaptation of, 132
    challenges of networked
        environments, 7
Critical infrastructure
    attacks against, 48–50
    as opportunity for crime, 57–58
Cryptography, 78–79
Cuckoo's Egg, The (Stoll), 10
Cyber Angels, 128
Cyber watchdog, 128
Cyber-extortion, 39
Cybercrime, *See also* Electronic crime
    basic trends, 76–82
    commercialization, 80–82
    cryptography, 78–79
    integration, 82
    juvenile involvement, 82–84
    sophistication, 76–78
    three factors, 55
    use of term, 2
Cyberterrorism, 45–48, 51–54
Cyberwarfare, 46-48
Cybervigilantes, 120–121, 127–131

"Dark figure" offenses, 61
Dark Market, 97
Data
    destruction or damage
        to, 6, 34
Data processing technology, 4
Data theft, 15, 81
Data-matching technologies, 87
"Datastream Cowboy", 10–11
Day trading, 25
Defense Advanced Research Projects
    Agency (DARPA), 89
Defenses, 99–100, 111–112, 122
Denial-of-service attacks, 34–35
    as dramatic crime, 9
    juvenile case, 82–84
    losses from, 34
    Port of Houston, 50, 111
Department of Homeland Security (US),
    40, 108, 126
Dictionary Attack, 36
Digital divide
    use of term, 55–56

Digital technology
    disadvantages, 1–2
    research uses of, 1
    restrictions on offenders, 116–119
Direct Marketing Association, 125
Disadvantages of digital technology, 1–2
Distributed denial-of-service (DDOS)
        attacks, 26, 34, 76
    defense, 111
    definition, 26
    Dreamboard, 108
Drink or Die piracy group, 19, 86, 107
Drug trafficking
    as computer-related crime, 67–68
Dumpster diving, 9

E-commerce
    complaints since 1998, 113, 136
    costs of crime, 69
    increasing volume of, 58
    losses to, 69
    online credit card fraud. 70
    privacy threats, 87–90
    spam and, 27, 35–36, 82, 125, 133–134
E-mail. *See* also Spam
        (unsolicited commercial e-mail)
    anonymous, 7, 32
    invitation to check out
        website, 37–39
    legislation, 133–134
    misadventures with, 63
    phishing, 36–39
E-mail addresses, sale of, 80
Eavesdropping, electronic, 95
Economic intelligence, 18
Electronic crime
    future of, 135–136
    use of term, 2
Electronic criminal havens, 75, 132
Embezzlement
    computer use in, 4–5
    fraud, 28
Encryption
    circumvention, 90
    credit card details, 15–16
    in criminal conspiracies, 44, 79
    definition, 32
    described, 44, 59

security uses, 79
    trends, 79
Encryption key
    loss of data, 29–30
    managing encrypted evidence, 94
Equity Funding scandal, 4
Espionage, 16–19
Etiquette, 121
Eurobarometer Surveys, 66
European Commission on Human
        Rights, 93
Evidence, digital
    basic issues, 99
    principles for handling, 98–99
Extortion, 39–40
    background, 8
    cyber-extortion, 39
    means used, 67
Eye scan techniques, 123

Facial recognition techniques, 123
Falun Gong, 41, 102
Fantasy defense, 112–113
FBI (Federal Bureau of Investigation), 40,
        94, 97, 102
    Carnivore data collection, 89
    Computer Analysis Response Team
        (CART), 99
    key logger system, 94
    survey, 64
Federal Guidelines for Searching and
        Seizing Computers (1994), 99
Fifth Amendment, 93
Financial crimes
    Internet phishing, 62
    motives, 57
    trends, 67
Fingerprint scanners, 123
First Law of Electronic Crime, 136
Foreign prosecution, 106
Forensic computing specialists, private, 92
Forensic practices, standardizing, 99–100
Forgery, 29
Fourth Amendment, 89, 93–95
Fraud, 19–22
    ATM fraud, 28, 131
    auction fraud, 25–26
    embezzlement,.28

Fraud (*Continued*)
    fraudulent ordering of goods, 24–25
    manipulation of stock prices, 25
    sales and investment fraud, 24
    technology-neutral language of laws, 131
    unauthorized funds transfer, 27

Gambling, online facilities, 41
Global positioning technology, 13, 45
Global reach of electronic crime, 2
Gonzalez, Albert , 91
Goods, fraudulent ordering of, 24–25
Google research tools
    example of, 88
Google search engines
    Internet pornography law, 90
    Gorshkov, Vasiliy, 102-103
Government
    Carnivore (DCS 1000) network
        collection technologies, 89
    privacy threats by. 87–90
    role of, 131
Guardians, absence of capable, 55, 59–60
Guardianship strategies, 123–124
Guilty pleas, 110

Hacker Crackdown, the(Sterling), 5
Hacker culture
    strategies to change, 121–122
"Hacker-for-hire", 80
Hackers
    celebrity status, 10
    folk-hero status of, 5
    mobile hackers, 79
    Phone Masters, 15
    Romanian online ordering, 25
    Use of term, 5
Hacking, 9–12, 26
    automated tools for, 9, 77
    counter-hacke r, 128
    definition, 9
    exemplary prosecutions, 113
    intelligent malware, 76
    motives, 56–57
    special skills enhancement and
        sentencing, 115–116
    use of term, 5
Hand geometry, 123

Happy Hardcore, 14–15
Hardening the target
    banks, 92
    measures, 58
    new technologies of access control,
        122–123
Health insurance fraud, 5
Hess, Markus, 16
History of electronic crime legislation, 6–7
History of electronic offending, 4–6

Illegal interception, 12–13
ILOVEYOU virus, 33, 36, 68, 69, 104, 131
    legislation, 131–132
Impacts of cybercrime, 68–71
Incidence of crime, 61
Incidental to offense, computer as, 8–9
Instrument, computer as, 8
Integration, 82
Intellectual property rights
    legislation, 6
    piracy, 19, 114
lntelligent malware, 26, 76
International cooperation, 134–135
    Council of Europe Cybercrime
        Convention, 132-134
    foreign prosecution, 106
    G8 plan, 134
Internet
    extreme relationships, 45
    pedophile solicitations, 45, 112
    revolution in high-tech crime, 5
    world regions by usage and
        population, 55–57
Internet Fraud Complaint Center
    (IFCC), 67
Internet of things, 136-7
Internet relay chat (IRC), 44, 107
Internet safety groups, 124, 128
Internet service provider (ISP)
    data retention policies, 129
    illegal use of services, 14–15
    law enforcement and, 13, 40
    requirements to assist governments, 126
    spam control, 124–125
    theft, 80–82
Investigation, 91–119
    adapting techniques to cyberspace, 132

Investment solicitations, fraudulent, 24, 36
Islamic State, 52, 53–54
Ivanov, Alexey, 102-103

Junk faxes, 135
jurisdictional issues, 103–105
Juvenile involvement, 82–84 *See also* Mafiaboy

Key logger system (KLS), 94
Key loggers
    definition, 32
    KGB, 16
"Kuji,", 10–11

Lashkar-e-Taiba, 51
Law enforcement
    data retention, 129
"Legion of Doom", 11
Legislation, 131–132
    e-mail, 125
    history of, 6–7
Levin, Vladimir, 27, 105
Loverspy program, 13
LulzSec, 97

Madoff, Bernard, 4
"Mafiaboy", 10, 34, 57, 104–105
    costs of attacks, 69
Mail bombing, 34
    of critical infrastructure, 48, 49–50
Malicious code, 33–34
    commercialization, 80–82
    defenition, 32
    as dramatic crime, 9
    impact of, 68
    sophistication, 76
    in spam, 82
Malware, 26, 76–77
Manning, Chelsea
    (Bradley), 30
Man in the Middle attack, 32
"Masters of Deception", 11
Melissa virus, 69
Misadventures, innocent explanations for, 63

Mitnick, Kevin
    background, 11
    post-release restrictions on, 117–118
Mobile hackers, 79
Mobile phone technology, 12–13
Money laundering, 41
Monsegur, Hector, 97
Morris, Robert, 5
Morris worm, 5, 126
Motion Picture Association
    DVD piracy, 126
Motives for cybercrime, 56–57

National security
    data theft, 15
    National Security Agency (NSA), 17, 30, 46, 69, 81, 90
Nature of investigations, 92–93
Neo-Nazi propaganda, 41
Netsafe, 124
Network scanning program definition, 32
New technologies
    impact of, 1–2
    News of the World, 12
Nigerian advance free fraud Ietter, 19–23
    nonreporting of, 61-62
NIMDA virus, 76
Nonreporting, 61
North Korea, 31, 42

Obscene telephone calls, 42
Offensive content, 41–42
    complaints, 67
    regulation42
    Onion Router (see TOR)
Online banking
    money laundering, 41
Operation Artus, 107
Operation Buccaneer, 107
Operation Cathedral, 107
Operation Cybersnare, 96
Operation Falcon, 108
Operation Olympic Games, 45-46, 71,82
Operation Onymous, 109
Operation Titstorm, 35
Opportunity
    defense strategies, 122–123
    Organized cybercrime, 84-87

Palm geometry, 123
Password crackers
  Definition, 32
Passwords, 9
Pedophiles, 45
Personal computer,
    significance of, 5
Pharming, 26
Phishing, 36–37, 67, 77
  botnets, 87
  definition, 26
  sophistication, 59
Phone Masters hacker group, 15
Phone phreakers, 14
Phrack, 14
Phreaking, 4
  low-tech alternative, 14
Piracy, 19
  civil remedies, 126–127
  music and Video, 126
  nations with highest and lowest
      rates, 70
  Operation Buccaneer, 107
  sentencing, 113–116
Police
  computer crime and, 63–65
  investigation interests, 92
Political communications, 134
Pornography law, 90
Privacy threats, 87–90
  Sources of, 87
Private citizens, 127–131
Private enforcement, 125–127
Programmers, falsification of data, 35
Proportionate sentencing, 114
Prosecution, 109–113
  defenses, 111
  exemplary prosecutions, 113
  foreign, 106
Psychological warfare, 52

Ransomware, 78
Reasons for electronic crime
  guardians, 59–60
  motives, 56–57
  opportunities, 57–59
  theoretical frameworks, 55
Rebellion motive, 57

Recording Industry Association of
    America (RIAA), 126
Remote search technologies, 94
Reno, Janet, 113
Revenge Pornography, 30
Revenge motive, 57
Romance Fraud, 20-21
Rootkit, definition, 33
Routine activity theory, 55–60, 121-124
  strategies listed, 55
Rule of law, 131–132

Sales and investment fraud, 24
Saudi Aramco, 29
Santayana, George, 137
Scanning technology and forgery, 29
Search and seizure, 93–96
  anti-crime activities of private citizens,
      127–131
Security, information
  capable guardianship, 123–124
  defense strategies, 122
  New Zealand, 124
  Pluralistic prevention, 124–125
  private enforcement, 125–127
Security law
  legislation citing threat of terrorism, 7
Security solutions software, 122
Sentencing, 113–116
  aims of punishment, 113
  child pornography, 16, 67, 72
  encryption offenses in Europe and
      Australia, 44
  hackers, 9
  juveniles, 82–84
  piracy, 114
  proportionate, 114
  restrictions on probation or parole,
      116–119
  special skills enhancement, 115–116
  U.S. Sentencing Commission, 114
Sex slavery, 88
Sexting, 42
Signature dynamics, 123
Silk Road, 14, 109
Snowden, Edward, 12, 17, 30, 69, 90
Social engineering, 9
Social Media, 6, 51-52, 58

Sony Pictures, 30-31
Sophistication of cybercrime, 78–79
South Carolina Criminal Code, 130, 131
Spam (unsolicited commercial e-mail), 7,
        22, 35–36, 82
    botnets, 87
    definition, 27
    investigations of, 35–36
    legislation, 133–134
    malicious code in, 33–34
    privacy threats, 87
    Spear Phishing, 27
Special skills enhancement, 115–116
Spim, 27
Spit, 27
Spoofing, definition, 33
Spyware, 33
    stalking with, 42–43
Stalking, 9, 42–43
    background, 13
    jurisdictional issues, 91
    State and State Sponsored
        Cybercrime, 2, 7, 12, 18,
        (See espionage)
Statistics, 64
Steganography
    in criminal conspiracies, 44–45
    definition, 33
*Steve Jackson Games, Inc. v. United States
    Secret Service* (1994), 92
Stock prices
    day trading, 25
    manipulation of, 25
Stoll, Clifford, 10
Stuxnet, 46-47, 77
Substantive criminal law, 131–132
System integrity, 122
System security
    as opportunity reduction, 58–59

Target of offense, computer as, 8
Target-hardening measures, 58,
        122–123
Targets or prospective victims, 57–58
Telecommunications technology, 4
    law enforcement and, 100
Telegraph, 4
Telemarketing fraud, 4

Telephone, 4
    illegal use of services, 14–15
    obscene telephone calls, 42–43
Terrorism, 48–54
    legislation citing threat of, 7
    technology as means to
        facilitate, 51-54
Terrorism Information Awarness
        Program, 89
Text messages
    to organize criminal activity, 44
Theft of data, 15–19
    espionage, 16–19
    theft of credit card details, 15–16
Theft of services, 14–15
TOR (The Onion Router), 79
Total Information Awareness
        Program, 89
Trade secrets, 17, 18
Transnational cybercrime cases, 103
Trojan Horse
    to catch child pornographer, 111
    definition, 33
    Port of Houston defense, 50, 111
    stalking with, 42–43
    surveys reporting, 70
Trojan Horse defense, 111–112
Types of cybercriminals, 82
Typing patterns, 123

Ulbricht, Ross William, (109)
Unauthorized access
    commercialization, 80–82
    defenses, 110–111
    as initial indicium, 91
    juvenile case, 82–84
    legislation, 6–7
    losses from, 67, 68
    "new" crimes, 8, 9
Unauthorized funds transfer, 27
United Kingdom
    Association of Chief Police
        Officers, 100
United Kingdom Biometrics Working
        Group, 123
United Nations Office of Drugs and Crime
        (UNODC), 64, 101, 135
United States v. Booker (2005), 114–115

United States v. Triumph Capital Group
     (2002), 99–100
United States Central Command, 52,
     53-54
U.S. Department of Justice, 90
     Computer Crime and Intellectual
          Property Section, 99
     data retention by ISPs, 100
U.S. Secret Service, 49, 98
U.S. Sentencing Commission, 114
USA Patriot Act (Public Law 107-56), 7

Victims, 73-75
Victimization surveys, 65, 74
Virus, 33
     Complaints, 67
     cost of, 68, 69
     definition, 27
     ILOVEYOU virus, 33, 36, 68, 69,
          104, 131
     losses from, 71
     scanners to combat, 29
     sophistication, 76–78

speed of, 76
     surveys reporting, 70, 72, 74
Voice recognition techniques, 123

War driving, 15, 79
Website defacement, 30
Websites
     counterfeiting, 36, 42, 43, 77, 116
White-collar delinquency, 84
Wireless access points ("hot spots"), 79
Wireless local area networks (LANs), 79
Wireless technology, 79
     credit card details, 43
Wiretapping, 95
Worms, 31–33
     Definition, 27
     first, 9
     joint investigations, 125
     Morris worm response, 126
     surveys reporting, 70
     Zero Day Exploits, 81

2600: The Hacker Quarterly, 14